𝕴ale Law Library Publications

NUMBER 10

PORTRAIT BUST OF CHIEF JUSTICE TAFT

# William Howard Taft

YALE PROFESSOR OF LAW

&

NEW HAVEN CITIZEN

AN ACADEMIC INTERLUDE
IN THE LIFE OF THE TWENTY-SEVENTH
PRESIDENT OF THE UNITED STATES
AND THE TENTH CHIEF JUSTICE
OF THE SUPREME COURT

By Frederick C. Hicks

NEW HAVEN
YALE UNIVERSITY PRESS
London · Humphrey Milford · Oxford University Press
1945

*20387*

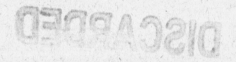

*Dedicated to the*

STUDENTS IN PROFESSOR TAFT'S CLASSES

*in Yale College and in*

*the Law School*

# PREFACE

*I talked with Mr. Taft only once, and that was when he was Secretary of War. This book, therefore, could not have been written by me without the help of many people. These include some of his former colleagues in Yale University, some of his former students in Yale College and in the Law School, and many of his other former friends and acquaintances still resident in New Haven. Their names are given in the following pages. To all of them I tender my grateful thanks. I am indebted also to several authors and publishers to whom credit is given in connection with the quotations that have been made with their permission.*

*My thanks go also to Mr. John Day Jackson for his willingness to have me quote extensively from the* New Haven Journal-Courier. *Add to these the records and publications of the University, its correspondence files, and the* Yale Daily News, *and the list of the sources from which have been drawn the items forming this mosaic is nearly complete.*

*Undoubtedly I have failed to apply for help to many individual persons who remember something which could have found a place in these pages. Now that the book is in print, I hope that those who read it will make known to me any additions that should be made.*

FREDERICK C. HICKS

# CONTENTS

# ILLUSTRATIONS

# INTRODUCTION

TURN about is fair play. Woodrow Wilson, the teacher, became President of the United States by defeating William Howard Taft. Then ex-President Taft became a professor.

For eight and a half years Taft bore this title at Yale University. He performed the duties of his professorship during six of these years, from April 1, 1913, to April 15, 1918, and from July, 1919, to June 30, 1920. He was on formal leave of absence from April 15, 1918, to June 30, 1919, and also during the academic year 1920–21.

Though no longer in public office, Taft the professor was still a public man. It was not possible for him to retire completely to academic seclusion. Nevertheless there was a new life for him at Yale and in New Haven, which is not part of his public life. This aspect of his years at Yale, Taft's biographers[1] pass by with brief notice. They write fully about the public official, the President, the ex-President in the public eye, and the Chief Justice, but not about the professor and the citizen of New Haven, both of which he was, not merely technically, but actually. From the point of view of his former associates in New Haven and in Yale University, this is an important omission, and it is important to anyone who wishes to form a complete picture of Taft. To fill in this gap is the purpose of the following pages.

1. Duffy, Herbert S., *William Howard Taft* (New York, Minton, Balch & Co., 1930); Pringle, Henry F., *Life and Times of William Howard Taft* (New York, Farrar and Rinehart, 1939), 2 vols.

# William Howard Taft

It was predicted that the remembrance of him as professor and as fellow New Haven citizen would be treasured. After the announcement had been made that his appointment to the Chief Justiceship had been confirmed by the Senate, the *New Haven Journal-Courier* (July 1, 1921) said editorially:

"We, his fellow citizens, are honored. . . . It is nothing short of remarkable that we should be living in the same town with one so unprecedentedly distinctive. In the old age of children now in the schools, eager listeners will press their questions:—'How did he look?' 'What did he say?' Scraps of paper with his signature will be sold in the auctions, and the incident of the chuckle, and what he did to reduce weight, and of his exchanges with Roosevelt, pleasant and otherwise, will be told and retold."

That prophecy has come true, even before the old age of children then in the schools.

# William Howard Taft

## I

## "I Am Coming Back to Yale"

WITHIN a few days after the election of Woodrow Wilson to the presidency, it was suggested that the Kent Professorship of Law in Yale College be offered to ex-President Taft. Although he had saved $100,000 during his term as President, he felt the need of choosing some means of supplementing his income. At first, he thought he would have to resume the practice of law in Cincinnati, but since he had been an officeholder since 1887, he doubted whether he was qualified for active practice. For another reason also, he hesitated to adopt a career which would necessitate his appearance in court. On March 4, 1913, after he had made his decision to become a professor, he told an interviewer for the *New York Sun* why he had decided against practice. "Six of the nine justices of the Supreme Court," he said, "bear my commission. Forty-five per cent of the federal judiciary have been appointed by me. That is the reason why I could not practice as an advocate. While you and I and the average man would know that this circumstance would not affect any court in any degree, the fact is that no matter how fairly a case might be decided, the inclination of the man who lost, if the side I represented won, would be to attribute the defeat to the fact that I had appointed the judge. That in itself is something that must be considered. What is needed these days is that nothing should be done that would ever give justification for even the appearance of a suspicion against the courts."[1]

The suggestion that a call be extended to Mr. Taft to become a professor at Yale originated with Anson Phelps Stokes, who at that time was Secretary of the University. At a meeting of the Yale Corporation which Taft attended in November, 1912, President Hadley broached the subject, and Taft took the proposal under consideration. On November 19, 1912, as shown by letters to his brothers, Charles P. and Horace D. Taft, Mr. Taft submitted the matter to his Cabinet. The letters, quoted in part by Pringle,[2] show how his mind was working.

"The duties are more than nominal," he wrote, "but they are very much what the professor wishes to make them. They involve a course of lectures to the senior class in the academic department on constitutional and governmental law, and such courses as he sees fit to give at the Law School. . . . They are quite disposed to let me do about as I please if I accept. . . . I suppose it is the advertisement or association of my name with the institution that they would like to cultivate. . . .

"This would take me away from Cincinnati, of course, and perhaps make me a resident of Connecticut in which I am about as much a political factor as I am in Ohio, which is very small. The proposition has some very attractive features about it. I do not retire to the practice of the law; I retire to the academic shades of Yale to teach it, and this very act takes me out of the maelstrom of politics. It is a dignified retirement, one

1. *New Haven Journal-Courier*, March 5, 1913.
2. Pringle, Henry F., *Life and Times of William Howard Taft*, p. 850.

which Cleveland had at Princeton, and one which would approve itself to the general sense of propriety of the country. The practice such as I would get would be incidental and it would attract less criticism. I submitted the matter to the Cabinet yesterday and they all thought it was an admirable suggestion and one that fitted itself remarkably well into the situation. . . . The only thing I do not like about it is that it takes me away from Cincinnati. . . . I forgot to say that the salary is $5,000 a year, which is the largest salary they pay. This would be enough for us to live on in New Haven with the income we have, and perhaps I could be reasonably certain to earn more to keep the wolf from the door, especially in view of the fact that I do not expect to eat so much after leaving the White House."[3]

The *Journal-Courier* of December 11 and 12 printed a rumor that the offer had been made, and on December 12 Stokes urged Taft by letter to think favorably of the proposal. "I want to take this opportunity," he wrote, "of telling you how earnestly I hope that you may act favorably on President Hadley's suggestion that you allow your name to be formally presented for the Kent Professorship of Law in Yale College. I feel that your presence in this University community would be an influence for good on every one of our thirty-three hundred students and that you would find New Haven an excellent center for such work of legal advice and of public service as might commend themselves to your judgment and which would not be inconsistent with the duties of your chair. The position

3. Taft to C. P. Taft, and to Horace D. Taft, November 20, 1912.

would be an honorable and dignified one and I am confident that both you and Mrs. Taft would find New Haven a delightful place in which to live. . . . Let me say incidentally that I know of two homes in quiet and dignified surroundings in the best section of New Haven, either of which would be available and desirable. Only three or four people in New Haven knew, up to yesterday, of the possibility of your coming and we have entirely refrained from bringing any pressure to bear upon graduates or members of the faculty to urge you to come, but as the suggestion for the extending of a call to you originated with me, I felt that I was quite at liberty to tell you how sincerely I hope that you may consider it favorably. . . . I feel that should you come to Yale, you could render here a public service worthy of comparison in the breadth of its influence with what you have done on the bench, in the Philippines, and in the highest posts of the government at Washington."

Taft replied from the White House on December 17, 1912, saying that he thought he should accept, and asking more information about the "house which is next to the Farnams, up on the hill. I should not like to go above $200 a month for rent. My present plan would be to go to New Haven at the opening of the spring term, and stay at the Taft Hotel until Commencement, then go to Murray Bay, and return to New Haven about the 15th of September to begin housekeeping. I should like a lease perhaps for two years, with the privilege of two more; or if I liked the house, I might take it for five years. . . . I am going down to Augusta for thirty days after the fourth of March, to play golf, and take a rest, and I should be ready, I hope, for work in the spring term, if I decide to go to New Haven. . . ."

The next day, December 18, 1912, it was announced in Washington that Taft had decided to accept the Yale offer. The reaction of the press of the country to this announcement was enthusiastically favorable. Comments from many newspapers were reprinted in the *Yale Daily News* of January 3, 1913, in which also the information was given that "Colonel I. M. Ullman, in whose hands the selection of the new professor's residence has been placed, has very carefully considered many sites, chiefly on Hillhouse and Whitney Avenues, and is now in Washington making his report."

The appointment of Mr. Taft to the Yale Faculty was carried out with customary formality. On January 4, 1913, President Hadley reported to the Prudential Committee that a tentative offer had been made, and on January 20, 1913, the Corporation duly elected him by ballot "Kent Professor of Law in Yale College at a salary of $5,000 a year, the appointment to take effect at his convenience this spring." Taft, a member of the Corporation, came to New Haven to attend this meeting. He was met at the station by Professor H. C. Emery, as representative of the Faculty, who escorted him to Woodbridge Hall. On January 23, Secretary Stokes formally notified Taft of his election, and on January 24, from the White House, Taft sent his acceptance of the appointment. In conclusion, he said that he would advise Mr. Stokes "by letter the day in March or April next when I can present myself and enter upon my duties."

Characteristically, Taft made his first public statement concerning his appointment in the form of a letter from the White House to the *Yale Daily News*, a student publication. It is full of sentiment for Yale, and of hope that he might be of service to the rising generation. It is herewith reprinted in full from the issue of February 25, 1913.

*"To the Editor of the Yale Daily News:*

"I am coming back to Yale. And I am coming with a sense of gratification which, I dare say, few can appreciate who have not had the privilege of being an undergraduate in the dear old University and then going out into the stress and turmoil of the world; for then it is that one looks back on his college days and realizes their advantages and their pleasures, and realizes them all the more keenly if they have been spent at Yale.

"A dozen times since I have been residing in the White House I have been back to Yale, and now that the election has come and gone I do not mind saying that each time I have gone back the charm of the dear old University has seemed more potent, more alluring. So, while I am now to return as a member of the Faculty instead of as a member of the collegiate body, or an alumnus, or a trustee, I venture to say that in the entire body there will be none with lighter heart or stronger hopes.

"It is not without some misgivings that I have accepted a professor's chair, not without a realization of the tests which the bright young men among the Seniors are apt to apply to one's knowledge of law, not without the knowledge that far more than on the bench is one's ignorance and forgetfulness likely to be exposed. And yet, despite these dangers, it is a great pleasure to me to think of coming back and talking to these very Seniors.

"It is with no great claim to erudition that I come back to Yale, but it is with the earnest hope that from a somewhat extensive and varied experience I may have gleaned something which may be of use to the young men with whom I shall come in almost daily contact. There is need of our universities. There is need that our young men should appreciate the Constitution of the United States, under which we have enjoyed so many blessings and under which we must work out our political and economic salvation. And this need is especially keen in a day when that instrument is regarded so lightly by a class of fanatical enthusiasts seeking short cuts to economic perfection, on the one hand, and by unscrupulous demagogues who to promote their own interests do not hesitate to inculcate disrespect and even contempt for the Constitution and the laws enacted under it, on the other.

"It is but natural that I should feel that the traditions and associations of old Yale form a peculiarly fitting soil in which to sow the seed and cultivate the flower of love of order, respect for law and veneration for the Constitution and its traditions. And if my study of the law, my eleven years on the Bench, my experience in the Philippines and my work in the cabinet and the Presidency shall have fitted me to lend some aid, however small, to carrying on the Yale spirit, in its broadest and truest sense, I shall be as happy at Yale as a professor as I was as an undergraduate.

"If I can help the men of Yale to know the value of our institutions and to appreciate the danger of accepting every nostrum that is offered and of abandoning those foundations without which our government could not have been, I will be thrice content.

"There is nothing in this view inconsistent with progress toward the highest ideals and the broadest equality of opportunity or with the promotion and spread of happiness among all the people. Indeed it is prompted only by well-founded anxiety lest in our search for short and easy cuts to general happiness that can only be attained by the continued practice of self-sacrificing virtues, we lose the progress we have made, the maintenance of which is the condition, and the essential condition of further progress.

Wm. H. Taft"

In a letter of November 20, 1912,[4] Taft referred to the possibility that he might give lectures in the Law School as well as in the College. Dean Henry Wade Rogers, of the Yale Law School, is quoted in the *Yale Daily News* of January 3, 1913, as saying: "While the professorship which he accepts is in the faculty of Yale College, I hope that when details of his work are finally agreed upon, it will be found that he has consented to give some part of his time to the instruction of law students." In order to assure this result, the Governing Board of the Law School, on February 15, 1913, passed a resolution which resulted in a vote by the University Corporation, February 17, 1913, authorizing the Prudential Committee to arrange a connection of ex-President Taft with the Law School. This Committee, on March 1, 1913, "Voted, to confirm the request of the Governing Board of the Law School that Hon. William H. Taft, LL.D., Kent Pro-

4. See ante, p. 2.

fessor of Law in Yale College, be also appointed Professor of Law in the former department. It is understood," the resolution continued, "that Mr. Taft will be a member of the general Faculty of the School but not of its Governing Board." On March 8, 1913, by letter to Secretary Stokes, Taft accepted this appointment.

Taft had been a Fellow of the Yale Corporation since 1906. At the Commencement of June, 1912, he had been reëlected an Alumni Fellow, receiving 3,231 out of a total of 3,263 votes cast. By letter of March 8, 1913, to President Hadley, he terminated that connection. "I beg herewith to tender my resignation as a member of the Yale Corporation—one of the six elected by the alumni of the University. I do this because I have accepted a position as Kent Professor of Law in Yale College, and I do not deem it in the interest of the University that a member of the Corporation should at the same time be a Professor under its appointment and in its employment. I understand the theory of the government of the College to be that the only relation between the Corporation and the Faculty shall be through the President."[5] Commenting on the resignation and its acceptance by the Corporation, Mr Stokes said: "This decision on the part of Professor Taft, following Professor [Simeon E.] Baldwin's action in consistently absenting himself from Corporation meetings for over two years in spite of his holding *ex-officio* membership as Governor of the State, has established a tradition which has nearly the force of law—that no person, except the President of the University, should

5. Report of the Secretary of the University, in President's *Report*, 1912–13, pp. 34–35.

at the same time render service as a member both of
a Yale Faculty and of the University Corporation."

There was nothing incongruous about the acceptance
by Taft of the appointment to teach law. He was a
graduate of a law school, having received his LL.B.
degree from the Law School of Cincinnati College in
1880. On May 5 of that year he was admitted to the
Ohio Bar, and in 1882 he formed the law firm of Lloyd
and Taft. His active practice lasted from 1880 to 1887,
but during that time he held several offices: from
January 3, 1881, to January, 1882, he was Assistant
Prosecutor of Hamilton County, Ohio; from January,
1882, to March, 1883, he was Collector of Internal
Revenue for the First Ohio District; and from 1885
to 1887, he was Assistant County Solicitor of Hamilton
County. From March, 1887, to 1890, he was Judge
of the Ohio Superior Court sitting in Cincinnati. Then
in January, 1890, he became Solicitor General of the
United States, on the appointment of President Harrison. He served in this office until March 17, 1892, when
the same President appointed him Judge of the United
States Circuit Court for the Sixth Circuit. The next
year he became Senior Judge in this Circuit, and he
served in that capacity until March 12, 1900, when
President McKinley appointed him Chairman of the
Philippine Commission.

This education and experience would not necessarily
have qualified Taft to teach law. He had, however,
had actual experience in teaching and in law school
administration. The Law School of Cincinnati College
had not prospered. It was not connected with the University of Cincinnati. The latter institution in June,
1896, organized its own school, the first class being

held in October, 1896. Taft was not only an organizer of this school, along with Judson Harmon, Lawrence Maxwell, and others, but he became its Dean, as well as its Professor of Real Property. In May, 1897, the Law School of Cincinnati College, which Taft had attended, and the new School of the University, of which he was Dean, were united. Taft administered the combined schools and taught his classes until his appointment to the Philippine Commission in 1900. For many years thereafter Taft's name appeared in the Law School's catalogue, with the appended note that he was "on leave." He took his law school work seriously, and never lost his interest in the school. On October 28, 1925, after he had become Chief Justice of the United States Supreme Court, he returned to Cincinnati to make the chief address at the dedication of the Alphonso Taft Hall, named after his father, which was about to be occupied by the University Law School. In his address he told of the advances that had been made while he was Dean, and spoke with approval of the adoption then of the case method of instruction.

It can be said with strict truth, I think, that Taft never regretted his decision to become a professor at Yale. It is undoubtedly true that he realized a life-long ambition when he became Chief Justice of the United States. But, short of that, he preferred to remain on at Yale in the capacity of a teacher. He did not desire an executive position either at Yale or elsewhere. In 1899, he had declined to be considered for the presidency of Yale University, and in 1913, he quashed the suggestion that he become Dean of the Yale Law School. In the years 1913, 1914, and 1915, there were rumors that he had been offered the presidency of Johns Hopkins University, of the College of the City of New York, of Lafayette College, of the University of Texas, and of Dartmouth College, respectively. He did his best to set all such rumors at rest. For example, on March 15, 1914, in a dispatch to George W. Marshall, President pro tempore of Delaware College, Newark, Delaware, he said: "I am quite content with my position in New Haven, and I could not accept the presidency of any university or college for two reasons, first, because I am not fitted for it, and second, because I have other work in which I believe I can do more good." Nevertheless rumors and suggestions persisted. In February, 1921, when the impending retirement of President Hadley was announced, it was urged that Taft serve as his successor, at least as an interim appointment.

Although he retained an active interest in politics, both local and national, he had no desire to run for elective office. When it was suggested in June, 1914, that he stand for Congress from the New Haven district, he replied that he was happy at Yale. Again in 1916, in response to questions about the candidates to be nominated in the Republican National Convention, at Philadelphia, he said: "I am now in a respectable profession. I hope to live and die a professor." In Chicago, August 28, 1916, to attend a bar association meeting, he told reporters that Chicago had convinced him that he was out of politics. "I walked four blocks through the downtown streets and made one purchase in a store without anyone apparently recognizing me." In a letter of April 26, 1920, addressed to David Herriott, of Chicago, who had urged Taft to become a candidate for President, he said:

"My attitude toward the treaty [of Versailles] has put such a proposal out of the range of practical possibilities." He advocated participation in the League of Nations regardless of political consequences to him. If the Chief Justiceship had not finally come his way, I think he would in fact have been glad to "live and die a professor."

This is so, despite the fact that his income from the University was very small compared to what he had previously earned. He liked the relationship and the associations, and the freedom that he had to lecture and to write. For three years, his salary as professor remained at $5,000. It was then increased to $6,000, and so remained for two years. On his return from leave, it was put at $4,000 for work done in one semester. I estimate that his total earnings at Yale amounted to a little more than $32,000, with an average of just over $5,000 a year. According to Pringle, he was earning that much in the practice of law in 1885. His salary as President of the United States was $75,000 with $25,000 more for expenses. Nevertheless, he was willing and apparently happy to work very hard, lecturing and writing, to supplement his Yale income.

His satisfaction in the new situation in which he found himself is summed up in spontaneous remarks that he made in All Souls' Church, Washington, D. C., after the service, on October 14, 1914: "The last sixteen months," he said, "have been as happy and full of comfort as any period in my life—the comfort of struggling to help along in a quiet, humble way—of being able to say what you choose and say only that which you really believe without reservation—is something that the previous experience in Washington in positions of responsibility makes you appreciate."[6]

6. *Journal-Courier*, October 19, 1914.

## II

## The "Royal Welcome"

Secretary Stokes kept the telegraph wires hot arranging for Taft's arrival in New Haven as a Yale professor. Taft had disapproved the proposal of the Governor's Foot Guard that the troop meet him at the station and escort him to the University. But he could not resist the desire of Yale students to stage a reception in their own way. There was to be a parade, and brief exercises on the campus, and therefore the exact time of arrival must be known. In response to one of Stokes's telegrams to Augusta, Georgia, Taft replied by letter of March 25, 1913, that he would arrive in New York on Monday, March 31, spend the night with his brother Henry, and come to New Haven Tuesday morning, on "any train that will be convenient for the boys. I had hoped to avoid any demonstration, but if the boys really desire it, of course I shall yield." The time of arrival was finally set for 12.00 noon, April 1, 1913.

The *Yale Daily News* of March 31 gave the places of assembly for the various groups of University students and the line of march to and from the station.

"The parade will start promptly at 11.30 rain or shine. Recitations, at 11.30 and 12.30 will be excused in Academic and Sheff. Men are requested to bring change, as a collection to pay for the band will be made during the march to the station. The marshals will be all 'Y' men in the University and the cheer leaders of last Fall." Academic seniors assembled at Osborn Hall on College Street; other classes at Phelps Gate. Sheff seniors met at Byers Hall; other classes at the corner of Grove and College Streets. The Law School met at Cheney and Ives Gateway, and the students of all other departments in front of the Divinity School on Elm Street. The line of march led down College Street to George and thence by Meadow, Water and State Streets to the station. The return trip would be by way of Meadow, Church, and Elm Streets, to Porter Gateway, and the University campus between Memorial and Woodbridge Halls. Memorial Hall was decorated with flags and bunting, as were also many buildings on the line of march.

The ubiquitous Stokes took an early train to Bridgeport, so that he might join the party there.

The spirit of the occasion is best grasped by reading the account of it which appeared in the *Journal-Courier* of April 2, 1913, under the display heading "Taft Receives Royal Welcome." The exuberance of this account would indicate that it was written by a student or by a young reporter glad of a chance to try his wings.

"Second to no triumphal procession of any Caesar and surpassing any such celebration in the history of the college of the bulldog was the return of William Howard Taft to this city yesterday, this time not with the anticipation of bright undergraduate years but with the honor due an ex-president and a Yale professor of constitutional law. The object of prolonged and, on the whole, favorable discussion throughout the country, and especially on the Yale campus, the event lacked nothing that could be given by the enthusiasm or numbers of the University men.

# The "Royal Welcome"

## More Than Half of College

"With the assurance of excused cuts, over one-half of the total registration of the University poured itself out onto College Street alongside the campus at 11.30, at the call of the martial strains of the Second Regiment band under the leadership of Frank Fichtl, in whose estimation the assemblage was 'the biggest ever in Yale.' Seven minutes from the first note on the horns the whole line had assembled and was on its way to the station. In the van marched the junior and senior 'Y' men of both the undergraduate departments. Close on the heels of these came the band, followed by the law school students under D. Tiggs. Then came the main body of the long array, and, in their joviality, its most active and representative part, the Academic and Sheff men, under the supervision of G. B. Cortelyou and A. W. Chauncey, respectively. J. R. Walker led the other paraders. The whole was marshaled by Captain Jesse Spalding of last year's eleven. 'Y' men, in white-lettered sweaters, served as the side guard, leading in the cheering, and acting in the capacity of intercollegiate police. The Sheff men, in a column four abreast, marched along side of the academics similarly arranged, so that it was a stream of eight men wide that stretched for at least a fifth of a mile. Passing the Hotel Taft in its splendid array of flags, the collegians filed on their way between living, waving hedges of awe-struck men and women and laughing windowed walls of surprised shop girls, for whom more than one cheer was set up.

## Collection of $130

"During this progressive lark a collection was conducted to defray the incidental expenses of the day:

this totaled $130, $15 of which, in excess of the necessary amount, will be given to the Ohio flood sufferers.

"Just before the station was reached the line swung across the loop formed by Water, State and Union Streets, where the immensity of the numbers could be clearly viewed. In front of the station itself ranks were doubled up to sixteen, in a single rank. But even this condensation of the length of the files was not sufficient to bring the rear guard into sight of the carriage door where the guest of honor was to appear. As a result a mad break was made by this ostracized portion for better standing room.

## *The Ex-President Comes*

"On the concourse of the station the crowds were less thick and it was not difficult to discern on the car platform, as the 12 o'clock train into New Haven from New York pulled slowly onto the first track, the tall figure of Secretary Stokes, who had met the new professor at Bridgeport, beckoning to someone in the interior of the train. When the engine finally came to rest Mr. Stokes was joined by the party beckoned to, Mr. Taft himself, who beamed jovially on the congregation around his path. Mrs. Taft, dressed entirely in black, soon followed her husband into view, when the couple descended to the concourse, where the party was met by greetings from Dean Rogers of the Law School, and Dean Jones of the College. The handshaking was interrupted by the sudden and precipitous arrival of Jesse Spalding, who, having been introduced to Mr. and Mrs. Taft, presented the only lady in the celebration with a large bunch of violets in behalf of the University. Brushing past the black boxes of the photogra-

TAFT'S GRADUATION PICTURE
YALE 1878

phers, the little group passed through the building out of the other side by way of the north exit.

### Pandemonium Breaks

"When the first glimpse of the arrival reached the mass outside there was pandemonium, for several minutes, over which the cheer leaders could prevail not in the least. Stopping as though thunder struck, the incoming member of the faculty hesitated and faced the huge audience in silence before he and Mrs. Taft entered the automobile that was to carry them to Memorial Hall for the address. Mrs. Taft took her place on the right of the back seat beside her husband. In front of them were Dean Jones, Dean Brown and Mr. Stokes. In the front seat was Treasurer Day, of the University, and the ex-President's private secretary, Mr. Mischler.

### The Procession

"As the auto moved slowly off, the former line of march was resumed, with the professorial party directly behind the band, which the hood of the machine constantly nosed into the production of a steady and sustained repertoire [sic]. As a special honorary bodyguard to the only vehicle in the procession, were the four captains of the major sport teams—Captain Blossom of the baseball team and Captain Snowdon of the crew, on the right, and Captain Wagoner of the track team and Captain Spalding of the football team on the left. As actual protection, however, there was a special detail of three detectives from headquarters, Ward, Dorman and Ledwith. Later, at the university campus part of the program, eight patrolmen were also in attendance.

"At the head of the triumphal march ranked the 'Y' men, D. M. Bomeisler, 1913; H. H. Ketcham, 1914; B. F. Avery, 1914; C. C. Brown, 1914; R. S. Cooney, 1914; P. G. Cornish, 1914; E. D. Davis, 1914; R. Dyer, 1914; C. Gile, 1914; R. A. Douglas, 1914; W. Harpman, 1914; W. Lippincott, 1914; W. C. Warren, Jr., 1914; N. W. Wheeler, 1914; L. Carter, 1915; T. H. Cornell, 1915; C. E. Clark, 1915; F. J. Loftus, 1915; H. Pumpelly, 1915; L. J. Arnold, Jr., 1914 S; D. Markle, 1914 S; J. Pendleton, 1914 S and N. S. Talbot, 1914 S. They were under the leadership of Captain Ketcham, of the 1913 football squad. One of the men also held, by a leash, the famous Yale bulldog, Beans, the property of William Howe.

"On Meadow Street near the armory the long line suddenly came to a halt, while Captain Wagoner, standing on the top of a street car just ahead, led in a long cheer for the guest of honor, ending with nine emphatic 'Tafts.'

### Up University Street

"At the Noah Porter memorial gateway the automobile of the encumbent [sic] professor stopped while the passengers disembarked for the march up University Street. The university campus was already crowded when the main body of spectators arrived there.

"As the future faculty member approached, the ovation increased a thousand-fold and continued in this way all the time the little party was on its way to Memorial Hall, from the balcony of which the address was to be made. While the prospective speaker was within the building, cheers were led by head cheer leader Harper and just before the speech, after the ex-presidential party had entered the balcony, which was draped with American and Yale flags, nine hearty 'Tafts' were almost screamed out by the seething mass below.

## President Taft's Speech

"The first words the new professor uttered in that capacity were as follows:

" 'Men of Yale, you will believe me when I tell you that I am greatly touched by this student demonstration. When it was suggested to me I deprecated it and thought it might be better to defer it until I took my departure, but as I hope that may be indefinitely postponed and as I hope Mrs. Taft and I are to become permanent citizens of the city and members of the faculty of Yale College, I thought it best to take what was coming to me at first.

" 'You may have heard more or less discussion when presidents of the United States are retired—voluntarily or otherwise—as to what should be done with them, to take care of them. When I took inventory all I had was a somewhat tarnished reputation as a lawyer; a profession that I had abandoned 30 years ago, but at the suggestion of President Hadley it was decided that what little law I have left might be put into practice here and I am here to again become an active Yale man. As I hear your cheers and songs I feel young again, as if I had shed some of my years.

" 'All this may seem egotistical to you, but I come here wanting to help what little I can the young men who are going out into the nation. I want to help preserve what part of the nation is worth preserving and without which the nation cannot exist. If I can do this I shall thank God for the opportunity.

" 'While I would not minimize Yale's spirit in my day I do feel that Yale is progressing and that her ideals are higher. The theory that a man has to go through some hell in order to get to heaven, those who have got to my years utterly reject. The Yale of today is a Yale of higher ideals and the morals among the student body today are higher.

" 'I am here to work in the ranks with you and to aid the President of the College who is now away from you, but I am thankful to say that recent information is that the great man will soon return to us in good health.

" 'I ask you to close this meeting with the benediction that you give us your heartfelt cheers and wishes for the early return to his office of Arthur Hadley.'

## Bright College Years

"The close of the address was the signal for fresh outbursts in the form of nine cheers, first for the speaker, and then for President Hadley. At the first strains of 'Bright College Years' every hat was immediately snatched off, and everyone, including the ex-President, joined in the praises of Eli Yale.

"When the crowd had scattered the newcomer descended the stairs of Memorial Hall, at the bottom of which he greeted some of his old friends, among them Colonel Norris G. Osborn. All but Deans Jones and Rogers got into the automobile which was in attendance at the front entrance of the hall, in which they

# The "Royal Welcome"

were whisked away to the Taft Hotel where luncheon was had, Mr. Taft partaking of his in his apartments."

This student demonstration and official Yale welcome were heartily enjoyed and approved by the town. In anticipation of Taft's arrival, the *Journal-Courier*, on the morning of April 1, said in an editorial extravagance: "If he wants to be mayor of it [New Haven], we will assure him an unanimous election. If he wants to be the board of aldermen, that too shall be his. We stand ready to strip any officer of our government of his gaudy raiment if Mr. Taft wants the job. . . . There is nothing too good for Bill Taft."

In an editorial on April 2, the same paper said that "Mr. Taft can do more to solve the sharp problems of undergraduate life [at Yale] by the sheer force of his personality and his love of high ideals than any other man connected with the teaching force."

From day to day, Taft's activities were carefully recorded—that on the evening of his first day at Yale, he invited Professor Henry C. Emery, whom he had appointed head of the Tariff Commission, to dine with him; that on the afternoons of April 3 and April 9, 1913, he played golf at the Country Club with Professor John K. Beach, of the Law School; that he dined with Professor Hiram Bingham on April 8; and that on the evening of April 3, he and Mrs. Taft attended a performance by the Boston Opera Company at the Hyperion Theater. The performance consisted of condensed versions of *Faust* and of *Martha*, and although the lighting was poor, the stage settings were worn, and there was only a piano accompaniment, Mr. Taft seemed to enjoy the performance; and that on April 13, he attended the services in Battell Chapel, and sat in the front pew in the northeast corner to the left of the choir.

He spoke briefly at the thirty-fifth annual banquet of the *Yale News* board of editors, on April 4, when Albert B. Crawford, 1913, acted as toastmaster, and Alfred Noyes read a poem. On Saturday, April 12, he was the guest of honor at a luncheon of the New Haven Chamber of Commerce, of which he had been elected a member on February 26, 1913. Colonel I. M. Ullman, the toastmaster, introduced Governor Simeon E. Baldwin, ex-Governor Rollin S. Woodruff, Justice John K. Beach, Mayor Frank J. Rice, George D. Watrous, Representative King, of Fairfield, and Professor W. H. Carmalt, as speakers to welcome Mr. Taft to New Haven. Mr. Taft replied in part:

"When asked to come here as a member, I had the idea that I might be given five or ten minutes to speak, generally, as a citizen of New Haven. And this involved on my part considerable assumption, considering my short time as a citizen. I am overwhelmed by these formal and very full measures of welcome tendered me by the distinguished citizens of Connecticut and New Haven.

"The profession of teaching is a very different one from law or the functions of a judge on the bench. I have cultivated highly that ability to look wise, and if that sufficed on the teacher's platform I should have an easy sailing. I have cultivated that heat of the advocate before court and I have shown that assumption of knowledge to a client, which a physician exhibits to his patient. I would be happy if these were all that was necessary.

"I am proud to be a citizen of New Haven. You have

your invaluable green surrounded by architectural monuments, you have East Rock and West Rock. You have diverse businesses which keep you prosperous and your people happy. Not all your eggs are in one basket. Perhaps your industries require skilled labor and doubtless you have that skilled labor. I think this might prompt you to organize industrial schools to create a supply of this skilled labor. The Italians and Russian Jews have come here since my time. Often they are looked upon as undesirable. I want to testify that they make good citizens, as loyal in appreciating and benefiting the institutions of this country as many Americans, who do not. You are having built a new post office. I know that the plan selected is good, for it meets the approval of George D. Seymour. We take our law through one man, our medicine through another, and I am willing to take my architecture through this citizen of New Haven.

"Of course, a city like this so near New York is compelled by competition to be active for its life. I am glad to stand in the ranks to help along. It is gratifying to find the life and pride of civic life and pride of university life so adjusted that they do not hinder each other but are rather a mutual assistance.

"I thank the gentlemen of various professions for your welcome. I have said more than I intended to say but I shall be satisfied if I have shown my appreciation of your welcome. If I can help along any who graduate at dear old Yale, I shall have realized my purpose in coming here."[1]

The next organization to honor him was the Governor's Foot Guard, 2d Company, which had made him an

1. *Yale Daily News*, April 14, 1913.

honorary member on March 6, 1913. There were two hundred present at the banquet on the evening of April 21, 1913, when Major Hewlett presided as toastmaster, and Governor Baldwin spoke. In the course of a graceful speech, Taft said: "I am glad to think that, for the present at least, I have every qualification for a place in this distinguished company. For the last twelve years, I have done nothing but encounter the dangers of official banquets. I lived through it, however, and now I have come to New Haven for rest. I am indeed a bottle-scarred [sic] veteran."

On April 11, 1913, it was announced that Taft would deliver a course of lectures on "Questions of Modern Government." These would be given in the Lampson Lyceum on Monday and Friday afternoons at five o'clock, beginning on May 2, 1913. As they were successively delivered, the lectures were separately commented upon and partly reported in the newspapers. The lectures in full were, in November, 1913, published by the Yale University Press, under the title *Popular Government, Its Essence, Its Permanence and Its Perils.* The author is described on the title page as "Kent Professor of Law, Yale University." In the brief introduction, Taft explained why he was called upon to give these lectures. "I came to Yale," he wrote, "to assume my duties as Kent Professor of Law near the end of the school year, when it was not practicable to add my courses of constitutional law to the then curriculum. It was suggested, therefore, that during the spring term, I prepare and deliver a course of lectures on some questions of modern government. This I did, making my text the preamble of the Constitution of the United States."

# The "Royal Welcome"

The delivery of these lectures gave Taft the first chance to grasp what he considered to be the chief opportunity offered by his professorship, namely, to instill into the minds of students respect for law, and to counteract the efforts of those "unscrupulous demagogues who to promote their own interests do not hesitate to inculcate disrespect and even contempt for the Constitution and the laws enacted under it." He wrote these words in his letter printed in the *Yale Daily News*, February 25, 1913, already quoted. He took his opportunity with evident pleasure and in complete confidence that it was better to stick to the tried and true, and have no dealings with doctrines and reforms then advocated by Theodore Roosevelt and his followers. "We have been accustomed," he said in his first lecture, "to muckracking in the case of living public men, but it is novel to impeach our institutions, which have stood the test of more than a century, by similar methods with reference to their founders, now long dead."

Only once did Taft go out of town to deliver an address. This was on May 30, 1913, when he spoke in New York City at the dedication in Columbus Circle of the monument in commemoration of the sinking of the battleship *Maine* in Havana Harbor, February 15, 1898.

The final event in Yale's welcome to Taft took place on June 18, 1913, at the alumni luncheon. His classmates of Yale, 1878, presented to the University an oil portrait of Taft, painted by August Franzen.[2]

2. This same class in 1941 presented to the Yale Law School another portrait of Taft, painted in 1914 by Sergeant Kendall, who was then Dean of the Yale School of the Fine Arts.

President Hadley (now restored to health) presided, and Judge Howard C. Hollister, of Cincinnati, made the presentation speech. Called upon to speak, Taft said: "You don't know, without experience, what a harbor of refuge from the sea of life this university has become."

So ended the first year. He had been welcomed by town and gown; he had settled down to academic life; and he had given a successful course of lectures. On June 30, 1913, the Tafts went to Murray Bay for the summer.

## III

## Professor in Yale College

That there should be a Professor of Law in Yale College, as distinct from the Law School of the University, was no novelty. From 1801 to 1810 Elizur Goodrich held such a professorship. He resigned because "the funds of the College would not allow the Corporation to give an adequate salary to their Professor." The post remained vacant until 1826, when David Daggett was appointed to fill it. Daggett, then sixty-two years old, had become a professor in the Staples Law School, predecessor of the Yale Law School, two years before. It was at Daggett's suggestion that the law professorship in the College was given the name "Kent Professorship of Law in Yale College," and was endowed, in 1833, by the allocation to its support of a part of the Centum Millia Fund.[1] Daggett was succeeded in the professorship in 1848 by Clark Bissell, and the latter by Henry Dutton, in 1855. Dutton died in office in 1869. Thereafter the professorship was vacant until Edward J. Phelps held it from 1881 to 1900. The only other incumbent up to the present has been Taft, who served from 1913 to 1921. All were men of importance in their time. Daggett was a United States Senator and Chief Justice of the Connecticut Supreme Court of Errors, Bissell and Dutton were Governors of Connecticut, and Phelps was Minister to Great Britain. All of them held professorships in

1. Hicks, F. C., *Yale Law School: the Founders and the Founders' Collection*, see Yale Law Library Publications, No. 1, pp. 39–42.

the Yale Law School (or its predecessor, the Staples Law School) at the same time that they held the Kent Professorship in the College.

Being a graduate of Yale College, and not of the Yale Law School, Taft's sentimental attachment was all with the College. He was pleased to return to it and wanted to take part in its activities. He wanted to be a professor among professors, and to be a friend and counselor to students. In his first month at Yale, at the request of E. W. Porter, president of the Yale Debating Society, he coached the Yale Freshman team in its preparation for the triangular debate with Harvard and Princeton. One night he worked with the team until nearly midnight. The question for debate was "Resolved that Cabinet officers should be given a seat and a vote in Congress."[2] Unfortunately Taft's coaching did not result in victory for Yale. The team that went to Princeton supported the affirmative of the question, and the team that stayed home argued for the negative against Harvard. Both Yale teams lost.

Taft attended Junior Proms, student banquets, smokers, and ball games, and took pains not to put a damper on student enthusiasms. He was thrilled when students made a demonstration at his house on Prospect Street, on the night of April 19, 1914, to protest the refusal of Huerta to salute the American flag. The *Journal-Courier* reported that "the collegians took the figurative fort by storm, trickling over the spacious lawn around the place in a solid converging stream whose goal was the red house on the summit of the mound." He quieted them by saying that the time had

2. *Journal-Courier*, April 28, 1913.

not come to declare war, and that the President has no power to do so. "I hardly need tell this fact to the 120 young men who attend my classes on constitutional law." He referred to this episode in an article which he wrote in 1916 on "Yale's Contribution to the Spanish-American War."[3] "Those of us who remember," he wrote, "that sultry spring night, two years ago, when, at the first sign of serious trouble in Mexico, fifteen hundred students suddenly began to parade around the Yale Campus, cheering the flag and the country, will not be surprised to learn that on the same kind of night, in the spring of 1898, there occurred a demonstration of almost the same sort. In fact, the two demonstrations were alike even to the details of calling upon President Hadley, then Professor Hadley, and Professor Phelps, for speeches upon the merits of a war." He saw in these student outbursts something more than signs of spring and of full spirit. "The truth," he wrote, "is that the college period of life is the one in which pure ideals are most easily aroused and the flame of patriotism evoked by danger to the country burns as intensely among college men as anywhere in the country."

He tried to understand the student point of view. Although he strongly disapproved of excessive drinking by alumni at Commencements and took part in a movement to eradicate this evil, he was inclined to be lenient with students who occasionally overstepped the bounds in this respect. He took a genuine interest in the personal problems of students. For example, when one of them was in serious difficulties with the

3. Nettleton, G. H., ed., *Book of the Yale Pageant* (New Haven, Yale University Press, 1916), pp. 122, 123, 126.

College authorities, and a committee of three, including Taft, had been appointed by President Hadley to investigate the case, Taft spent an hour in private conversation with the student, trying to get at the cause of the trouble. He was one of those who thought that the rule prohibiting undergraduate marriages should be relaxed. He was paternal to students, and eager to help them. Morris Hadley, who was one of his students, wrote of him[4] that "Mr. Taft was always kindness itself wherever students were concerned. When the United States went into the war in 1917, I suppose every student who had sat in one of Mr. Taft's classes, whether they had ever studied or not, together with a great many others who had never even had that connection with Mr. Taft, went to him for a letter of recommendation to the authorities making up the rolls for the first officers' training camps. He must have written hundreds of letters for Yale undergraduates and recent graduates."

His relations with the members of the College Faculty were pleasant and informal. He was already well acquainted with some of them. President Hadley of the Class of 1876 was in college when Taft was, and he had had a long association with him on the Corporation. He soon came to address his colleagues by their first names, or as "Brother" This, or "Brother" That. If one of them had a well-known aversion for something, he would joke with him about it. A case in point is "Brother" Albert G. Keller's distaste for ethics. Taft attended College Faculty meetings at first with considerable regularity, and went to some trouble to do so. On December 2, 1915, he made a special trip

4. Hadley to Frederick C. Hicks, June 19, 1940.

from Lawrence, Massachusetts, in order to be present. Many a meeting started off with a joke which did not become trite. Dean Jones would say: "The Presidential row will now be in order." The three presidents were Hadley, ex-President Taft, and Ernest Fox Nichols, who had been President of Dartmouth College, and who was Professor of Physics at Yale, 1915–20. Taft played golf with some of the Faculty members, among them the late William Lyon Phelps.

He acquired a strong feeling of respect and affection for Dean Frederick S. Jones. In a letter written to President Angell, June 12, 1925, regretting his inability to speak at the alumni luncheon of that year, and declining to serve longer as a Fellow of the Yale Corporation, he paid Jones the following tribute: "I am sorry this year not to be present to speak at the coming retirement of my dear friend, Fred Jones, from the Deanship of the College.[5] Few people realize how much the College owes to him for its material growth and for keeping high and pure the college feeling. He has given the best part of his life to this. Responsible for the discipline of the undergraduates, charged with guiding them in their selection of courses, knowing more about all of their personal life than any one else of the College authorities, he has been loyal and kept his charges loyal to the best traditions of Old Yale. How large a part he has played in the Harkness memorials and the other monuments that are now to frame forever future sweet Yale memories, many persons know, and I am glad to emphasize. I wish to say this as I am ending my official relation with the University."

5. Jones retired in 1927.

# William Howard Taft

He did not narrowly interpret his obligations to the College, to other departments, and to the University as a whole. He exerted his influence strongly to benefit the institution, and gave personal attention to many matters on which his advice and active help were requested. In 1914 and 1915 he spoke at meetings and dinners held to raise money for the Yale Medical School, and he wrote letters asking for contributions for this purpose. He represented the University at the first and second World Court Congresses, in 1915 and 1916, and he represented it also at the meeting of the Association of American Universities at the University of California, August 27–28, 1915.

On several occasions he was asked to give his opinion on the merits of manuscripts submitted for publication by the Yale University Press. One question submitted to him was whether the publication by the Press of a Protestant Encyclopedia would be apt to present Yale to the public exclusively as a sectarian Protestant university. He examined the question at some length in a letter addressed to Secretary Stokes, December 2, 1913, in which he concluded that no such implication could be made if the work were published. Nevertheless, the Encyclopedia was never published. On April 28, 1917, in Washington, D. C., he conferred with Secretary of War Newton D. Baker, on "military units training here at Yale." He entertained at his home notable visitors to the University, advised Secretary Stokes on rules of precedence at functions involving government officials,[6] attended receptions and conferences at Yale, and when he could not be present, sent letters to be read. An example is a letter to Stokes, dated

6. Taft to Stokes, June 13, 1913.

# Professor in Yale College

January 11, 1916, read in Spanish translation by Professor Hiram Bingham at a luncheon in honor of visiting members of the Pan-American Scientific Congress.

It was a foregone conclusion that he would be a speaker at alumni luncheons, and he was expected to shine. In response to an invitation from Stokes to speak in June, 1914, Taft on June 14, 1914, accepted, "but," he said, "to start a man off with the statement that he is 'to make the best speech of the afternoon,' is to put him in a condition of helplessness, and frighten him away from the platform. However, I shall be on hand under the sounding board, to back up the institution." He spoke at Yale on many other occasions, and only once did he fail to keep his appointment. In a letter to Stokes, November 29, 1917, explaining that delayed trains prevented him from arriving in time to speak in Woolsey Hall on Thanksgiving Day, he said: "I am much humiliated in finding that I was to be the *pièce de résistance*, and that my failure to appear was much more conspicuous than I had hoped it would be." He was in truth a great drawing card at Yale and with New Haven citizens. Two quotations will attest this fact. The *Yale Daily News*, of December 14, 1920, said: "Last night, Fritz Kreisler gave his annual New Haven concert in Woolsey Hall. As usual the auditorium was packed. It was an odd commentary that William H. Taft and this great violinist are the two personalities who have 'played' to standing room only this fall in Woolsey." The other quotation is from a letter written by Judson J. McKim to Frederick C. Hicks, May 13, 1940. Mr. McKim, who is now general secretary of the Cincinnati Young Men's Christian

Association, held a similar position in New Haven in Taft's time. In this connection he was associated with Mr. Taft in organizing the Red Cross and Liberty Loan drives. "The plan was," he wrote, "to have an opening dinner with some out-of-town speaker to arouse the enthusiasm of the general public. In New Haven we discovered, however, an interesting fact, namely, that we had two of our own local citizens whose appearance upon one of these drive programs brought out a larger attendance of local people than we could secure by bringing in an outsider, whoever he might be. These two men were, first, William Howard Taft, and second, Dean Charles Reynolds Brown, of the Yale Divinity School."

There was one thing that Secretary Stokes could not induce Mr. Taft to do for the University. He would not preach a sermon. On May 4, 1914, he replied to Stokes: "I have yours of May 2, asking me to preach at Yale. I shall see you and talk to you about it." This was the typed letter. At the bottom was written in Taft's hand: "I am afraid I am not sure enough of myself yet." A year later, April 29, 1915, Stokes returned to the attack. Taft replied on May 1, 1915: "You will have to excuse me," he wrote, "from filling the College Pulpit for some years to come. I don't feel that I am worthy to take that place, and I don't feel that I ought to. I am glad to take part in any College activity that I am fitted for, but a sermon is quite beyond me. I am sorry to disappoint you, but this is a sincere expression."

Incidentally, it may be said that he was ever careful that the fact that he was a Unitarian might not embarrass any institution or organization with which he was connected. Pringle (pp. 373-374) tells of the distortion of fact concerning his religious belief when he was a candidate for President in 1908; and Louise Randall Pierson, in *Roughly Speaking*,[7] says that she broke off relations with one of her admirers, because "he wrote me a letter saying that as Taft who was running for President, was a Unitarian, he and his family were *praying* for him." In January, 1899, Taft declined to be considered a candidate for the Yale presidency, partly because he feared that his religious affiliations might alienate the support of some of Yale's well-to-do contributors. He held consistently to his faith throughout his life, and he took part in the management of the denomination to which he belonged. On May 24, 1914, he was elected Honorary President of the American Unitarian Association, and on October 15, 1919, he was President of the Unitarian General Conference in Baltimore. But he did not try to make converts to his way of thinking. Mrs. Taft was an Episcopalian. He was so liberal in his views that he was acceptable as a speaker to all sorts of religious organizations, Protestant, Roman Catholic, and Jewish. A great many of his addresses were delivered before clubs associated with churches. His feeling for religion, and for the right of every person to worship in his own way, is clearly reflected in an address which he made in New Haven, on May 28, 1916, at the Universalist Church of the Messiah. The subject was Liberalism. Asserting that religion is necessary to man, he continued: "There have been many men who have been strictly moral but yet had no religious faith. But with most men, religion is essential

7. New York, Simon and Schuster, 1943, p. 35.

to moral impulse. It makes them have a sense of
responsibility towards God, whose authority they
recognize, and whose goodness they feel. I am a Unitarian, but Unitarianism and Universalism are in a
sense first cousins. They both come under the category
of liberal religions. . . . We can remember the time when
the Universalist and the Unitarian carried with him
something of the feeling of being on the outside, a
feeling that we were a peculiar people. I think that
that day has passed away."

In his relations with the College Faculty, and with
the University administration, and in his extracur-
ricular contacts with College students, Taft was a
decided success. In the College classroom also, his
appointment was justified by results, but this was not
because he was a "good" teacher in the orthodox sense.
When he tried to conduct his classes by the recitation
method which he probably recalled from his own college undergraduate days, his performance was, as one
student has said, surprisingly dull. But, as will presently appear, he eventually broke away from this
method, with the result that the weekly visits to his
classes became inspiring experiences. To arrive at this
end, he had to go through some amusing stages.

One of his difficulties was a tendency to be late for
classes. He never got over this, and it became necessary
for Dean Jones to tell the students that they must not
take "runs" on Mr. Taft, but must wait for him, at
least to the extent of fifteen minutes. "We filled in the
time when he was late," one student recalls, "by
shouting Yale songs at the top of our lungs. What the
rest of the professors in Osborn Hall thought of this
performance, we never found out." He usually did

arrive, and he took note of Corporation regulations, in order that he might comply with them. For example, on November 25, 1913, he received from Secretary Stokes a circular letter to the Faculty, containing the following: "Resolved, that no arrangements for regular teaching work elsewhere during the University year should be made by a member of the Faculty without the approval in advance of his Dean or Director, and that the conditions under which such work is undertaken should be duly reported to the Prudential Committee." The very next day, he wrote Stokes a long letter listing his out-of-town lecture engagements for the year 1914. "None of these lectures," he wrote, "involves my being absent from New Haven on days when I have lectures in either Yale College or the Law School, except the lectures which I have agreed to deliver at the University of Minnesota, when I shall be absent on two of my lecture days at Yale. I presume that lectures of this kind are not regarded as within the expression 'regular teaching work,' but I thought it well to advise you formally of the arrangements I have made. I have sent a similar letter to Dean Jones and Dean Rogers."

His College lectures were given in A1 Osborn Hall, two days a week throughout the year. The course was an elective for seniors and at first as many as 120 students elected it. In later years, the number was much smaller, but this was partly due to the disruption of college life by World War I. The College catalogue of the time says that the course would deal with "general constitutional law, with special reference to the Federal constitution," and that it would be conducted by means of lectures and textbooks. The book used was

# William Howard Taft

Emlin McClain's *Constitutional Law in the United States*.[8]

When the novelty wore off of having a former President of the United States as a teacher, students began to take advantage of his inexperience, and of his rather guileless assumption that all were there solely for serious purposes. Disappointed in finding that Taft intended methodically to have students recite, some of them sought means to avoid the necessity of preparation. Obviously, in a large class, a student could not be called upon every day. What were the chances of escape on any given day? Emerson Tuttle, one of his students in the Class of 1914, now Professor and Master of Davenport College at Yale, tells how they worked it out, and how a change of method came about.[9]

"The sheet of paper which contained our names was so large that for convenient handling it had to be folded at the middle and it was therefore obvious when he flopped the paper on the little table which stood in front of his chair as to which section of the alphabet he was looking at, and even with the certainty that the lots would fall among one half of the class, the chances of reciting were ten to one against being called upon. Furthermore, Mr. Taft did not mark the recitations. The result was a rather dull, uninteresting performance. It got so bad finally that Kenneth L. Moore and myself appointed ourselves as a committee to call upon Mr. Taft in his office in the Hotel Taft and explain the situation to him. We even went so far as to confide to him the practice of the gamblers in the

8. New York, Longmans, Green & Co.
9. Tuttle to Hicks, April 24, 1940.

back row, which was to offer insurance rates against being called upon and to raise or lower the rates according to whether he flopped or did not flop the large sheet of paper which contained our names. At this Mr. Taft threw back his head and began that high falsetto chuckle which delighted us all. He then said to me: 'I know things have been going rather badly. This morning there was a young man whom I called upon that didn't even know what *ancillary legislation* was.' I was greatly embarrassed but I confessed to Mr. Taft that I was the man, and I added: 'This proves my point, for, had I known I would receive a zero for my failure, I should have been prepared.' We made the suggestion that Mr. Taft conduct the course as a lecture course with ten-minute papers as a check on undergraduate preparation. He inquired how he would ever get the papers corrected, and we boldly, and without authority, said Dean Jones would provide readers for him. He laughed heartily and said: 'Gentlemen, I will try the experiment for two weeks.' Fortunately for us the first lecture was delivered at the time that Bryan, the Secretary of State, was traveling out to California to try to ease the situation then arising because legislation just passed or in preparation by the Legislature of that State, infringed upon certain treaty rights which the Congress of the United States had guaranteed to the Japanese. Mr. Taft enjoyed the situation. There were no ill-natured jabs at 'Brother Bryan.' His attitude was merely the ripe post-Jovian enjoyment of a President out of power who watches an opposition theorist go into action.

"The lecture was a masterpiece, and Mr. Taft was clapped to the echo—one of the first times I ever heard a lecturer clapped in course. This sealed the fate of the recitation."

Kenneth L. Moore, B.A. 1914, referring to his call with Tuttle on Mr. Taft, says:[10] "What certainly impressed me most was how very nice the ex-President was to us young squirts, and the fact that he was ready to follow our uninvited advice."

The system of class papers which was then in vogue at Yale, and which Taft was supposed to adopt, is described by Morris Hadley, B.A. 1916, as follows:[11]

"The students received an assignment at each lecture to be prepared by the following period, say twenty pages in some text book. When the next period arrived and you entered the lecture hall, you went to your regularly assigned seat, which carried a number. Seats were equipped with broad arms on which you could write. You found a sheet of paper there, on which you wrote your name and your seat number. The professor then stepped to the blackboard, which up to that point was concealed by a roller shade of the sort you find on windows. Rolling up the shade, two questions would be disclosed on the blackboard, one marked 'Odd' and the other 'Even.' These questions were based on the current assignment, or on something brought out in the previous lecture. You took the question appropriate to your seat number, and wrote hastily for five minutes. When time was up, the papers were passed along the rows to an assistant in the aisle who collected them. This five-minute chore out of the way, the professor then started on his lecture. Harvard men always held this Yale scheme up

10. Moore to Hicks, March 13, 1943.
11. Hadley to Hicks, June 26, 1940.

to scorn and derision, but it had its advantages. The student's mark at the end of the year was based on some sort of weighted average between the daily papers and the final examination, the proportionate weight varying with different courses."

Taft left out two essentials of this plan, viz., he did not assign seats, and he did not keep the questions on the blackboard covered until the moment when the test was to begin. In a letter of June 19, 1940, Morris Hadley tells what the result was:

"As an instance of the delightful inefficiency with which the course was run, I recall the fact that no seats were ever assigned. Each period started with the usual brief written test on some item in the assignment. Students who were unprepared would scramble for seats strategically located near to classmates who presumably were prepared. I think more copying of papers went on in that class than in any other which I attended during my four years. The authorities must have noted the fact, because after about a month Mr. Taft announced that the Dean's office had informed him that it was customary to put two questions on the blackboard, one for students occupying odd-numbered seats, and the other for students occupying even-numbered seats. Thereafter we always had two questions, one marked 'Odd' and the other 'Even.' As Mr. Taft still assigned no seats, the result was that each student would come into the room, decide which question would be easier, and then hunt up a seat appropriately numbered, in order that he could write the seat number at the top of his paper and answer the question of his choice. On days when one question was much easier than the other, the class would be dotted all over the room, with no even seats (or odd seats, as the case might be) occupied. As the room was large, and the class only half filled it, it was always possible to find a seat of the category desired.

"As far as I know Mr. Taft remained unconscious of what was going on, although on one occasion he did make a passing reference to the matter. As nearly as I recall his words he said:

" 'One of your number has felt called upon to inform me that a certain amount of cribbing goes on in this class. I am sorry to learn of this, and trust it is not as widespread as my informant believed. To go to college and then not take the trouble to prepare your lessons is a foolish thing. When your children come to go to college you will find it hard to reconcile such practices on your part with the standards which you will wish them to follow when in college. But, gentlemen (and here came his delightful anticipatory chuckle), when you get to be as old as I am you will have observed that a man who cheats generally does so because he needs to.'

"These incidents present the course in an unfair light, because to the minority of students who were really interested, it was an inspiration to listen to Mr. Taft, and observe his marvelous objectivity. I recall on one occasion when he referred to a matter then pending before the United States Supreme Court, where the constitutionality of a given piece of legislation was under consideration. After describing the matter with the same calmness as if it had taken place in the days of Washington or Jefferson, he added:

" 'This case is perhaps of particular interest to me, because I vetoed this bill on the ground that it did not accord with the Constitution, and it was passed over my veto.' "

Taft prepared no formal lectures for his College course, but relied on notes and headings which he drew up in long hand. His outline followed closely the divisions of the textbook. After he had adopted the ten-minute paper method above referred to, he dictated to his secretary the questions to be written about, and these each day were copied onto the blackboard by students assigned for that purpose.

The students whom he selected to mark papers were law students. Among them were Herschel Arant, B.A. 1911, LL.B. 1915, and in the year 1915–16 William W. Gager, B.A. 1913, LL.B. 1916. Before this arrangement was made, he took the papers with him on his long lecture trips in the second half of each week, and attempted to grade them on the train, in hotels, and at private homes where he was a guest. As there were at first over 200 of these papers a week, and at the lowest never less than 120 a week, the task was more than he could do under the circumstances. Many another teacher will sympathize with him as they visualize an ex-President of the United States driving himself to do justice to a crowd of students by giving personal attention to the papers of every one of them, forcing his mind to the monotonous task during every moment of escape from actual contact with persons about him. Even after he had turned the work over to assistants, he had the marked papers returned to him, and kept close track of the progress of his classes. He always himself drew up the final examination questions for all of his classes.

# IV

## Professor in Yale Law School

When Taft came to Yale in 1913, the arrangement for a combined academic and law course was already in effect. If a College senior intended to enter the Law School, he could elect to take not less than eight hours of work in the Law School, and thus, as stated in the University catalogue, obtain a credit for these hours "on the sixty hours required for the degree in Arts, and on the forty-one required for the degree in Law." Students who earned this credit while they were in the College were enabled to complete the Law School course in two additional years, or six years in all. Neither of Taft's courses, that in the College and that in the Law School, was involved in this arrangement. As Dean Rogers explained,[1] "The Academic course is credited only on the Academic degree and not on the Law degree. The course in the Law School is credited on the Law degree and not on the Arts degree. It is no part of the eight hours of law work open to election by Academic seniors."

The purpose of Taft's course in the College was not to train lawyers, but to add to the general culture and information of the academic student, in exactly the way that a course in history, economics, or literature might be expected to do. It was an elective course. His course in the Law School was, however, deemed to be an essential part of the law student's training, and it was for three years (1913–16), a required course for third-year law students. Why it ceased to be re-

1. *Yale Daily News*, April 8, 1913.

quired, beginning in 1916–17, can only be surmised. It is not an improbable supposition that students who had elected Taft's College course, and who later decided to enter the Law School, objected to being required to take a second course on the same subject by the same man, however eminent he might be, and even though the content of the two courses was not identical.

The Law School course in Constitutional Law, which Taft gave in Hendrie Hall, is described in the Law School bulletin, 1913–14, as follows:

"The constitutions of government, the making and changing [of] written constitutions, the three departments of government, the jurisdiction of the United States, citizenship, fundamental civil and political rights, legislative power, the police power, the right of eminent domain, the limits of the power to tax, the regulation of foreign and interstate commerce, *ex post facto* and retroactive laws, are the leading subjects considered."

From time to time the description was altered. That for 1916–17 read:

"The distinction between the federal legislative, executive and judicial powers; government of territories and insular possessions; the general relation of states and nation; express limitations upon the powers of the federal and state governments; due process of law and kindred topics; the regulation of foreign and interstate commerce."

In 1913–14, the case book used was Thayer's *Cases on Constitutional Law*. In subsequent years, Wambaugh's *Cases on Constitutional Law* was used.

For many years the Law School course in American Constitutional Law had been given by Simeon E.

Baldwin. Before it was known that Taft was coming
to Yale, Baldwin had asked to be relieved of the course
and his title had been changed from Professor of
American Constitutional Law and Private International Law to Professor of Law. The professorship
in Constitutional Law was assigned to George Dutton
Watrous, and it so appears for the year 1912 only in
the *Historical Record of Yale University*. Watrous had
never taught the subject, and he was therefore given
a year in which to prepare for his new course. Before
that year was up, Taft came to Yale. He was first
appointed in the Law School, with the title Professor
of Law. Everyone, including Watrous, recognized the
appropriateness of asking Taft to teach Constitutional
Law, and so Watrous withdrew, resuming his former
title of Professor of Law, while Taft by vote of the
Corporation, March 17, 1913, became Professor of
Constitutional Law. The friendly relationship between
the two men is shown in a letter written by Mr.
Watrous on March 29, 1940. "Shortly after Mr. Taft's
appointment," wrote Watrous, "he drove out to my
house in Woodbridge one cold, rainy, cheerless day,
to ask how I had intended to conduct the teaching. Unfortunately I was not at home. I saw him later and
told him how I had intended to teach, and he expressed the hope that he had not crowded me out. I
assured him that there was not the slightest doubt as
to the propriety of my withdrawal. It is perhaps fortunate," Watrous continued with characteristic mod-
esty, "that I did not teach, for the Constitutional Law
which I then would have taught is very different from
that now handed out by our Supreme Court, and my
students, if any, would probably have looked back

HILLCREST, 367 PROSPECT STREET
THE TAFT RESIDENCE FROM 1913 TO 1918

upon my teaching, and thought I knew nothing about the subject, which would have been more or less correct."

The only other course that Taft ever taught in the Law School was International Law which he gave in the year 1916–17 only, one hour a week throughout the year, to third-year students. He received an additional $1,000 for this work. The course was described in the Law School bulletin, 1916–17, as follows:

"The general principles of the subject as developed by treaties and conventions and by the common usage of nations. Special attention will be given to present-day problems. Probably Scott's *Cases on International Law.*"

When Taft came to the Law School in 1913, Theodore S. Woolsey had already become Professor of International Law, Emeritus. From 1912–13 through 1915–16, the only work offered in Public International Law was a course for graduate students to be given by Gordon E. Sherman, Assistant Professor of Comparative and International Law. Professor Sherman's connection with the school ended in 1916. Taft then gave the course above referred to, in the year 1916–17, but for third-year students only. He, however, supervised the work of at least one graduate student. In the following year Professor Edwin Borchard, who joined the Law Faculty in 1917, took over the course and gave it three hours a week during the first semester. This latter course was open to graduate students also.

Taft was probably asked to give the course because of interest in the subject excited by the probability that the United States would enter the European war, and because of his wide experience in international affairs. Next year the College followed suit. The report of Dean Frederick S. Jones, of the College, for 1916–17 (p. 176) says:

"International Law, which was formerly open to undergraduates is not now offered to them in the Law School, and by vote of the Faculty Professor Taft was requested to offer a course open to members of the Senior Class. Accordingly Law A1 will hereafter include General Constitutional Law and International Law. This course will not be counted toward the LL.B. degree."

Under this arrangement, as shown by the College catalogue, 1917–18, Taft did not give a separate course in International Law in the College, but squeezed the subject into the course, two hours a week throughout the year, which he had been giving as Kent Professor of Law. He included International Law in his College course during only one year, 1917–18. The next year he was on leave.

The number of students in Taft's class in Constitutional Law in the Law School was never large. During the first three years, 1913–14 to 1915–16, when the course was required to be taken by third-year men, the number of third-year students in the school, according to the Law School bulletin was, respectively, 30, 41, and 45. After that the course was made an elective. In 1917–18 less than a dozen students elected it. But the war years were a low point not only for the course but for the school; there were, for instance, only eight men in the third-year class in 1918–19. During this year Taft was on leave of absence and Professor Borchard gave the course. Two reasons account for the small enrollment in the school. First, in 1911–12, a rule had gone into effect requiring for entrance to the Law School the possession of a college degree (except for Yale College students who were taking the combined course), and this requirement had by 1913–14 materially reduced the number of students who had reached the third year. Second, the European war, even before the United States entered it, prevented students from entering the school, or caused them to drop out. Taft was a member of the Law Faculty during a critical period for the school, a period when a successful attempt was being made to raise the standards of the school, even to the accompaniment of war.

Those who were students in his law classes have vivid recollections of him. They recall how he conducted his course, and what made it interesting to them. Judge Carroll C. Hincks, LL.B. 1914, who was in Taft's first Law School class,[2] writes that "sometimes he would call on individual members to recite; sometimes he would assign a question for a ten-minute written paper. But generally before the hour was up he was talking freely. Sometimes, after a recitation on a particular case, he would describe the judge who wrote the decision, frequently embellishing his description with some pertinent personal anecdotes, and it seemed as though almost every question of Constitutional Law he would eventually illustrate out of his great wealth of personal experience.

"I recall that he insisted that we all memorize the Constitution, and at the close of the year presented each member of the class with a diminutive edition of the Constitution with his autographed card.

"He did not pursue the analysis of the cases which

2. Hincks to Hicks, April 9, 1940.

20387

we studied to any such degree as was the custom of other professors. As I look back on it, I don't think he developed the critical and analytical capacities of the students as some of our other instructors did. But he unfailingly made each hour of class a delightful experience. And in general he left us with the impression that cases apparently conflicting could be reconciled by some process of logic, although in the classroom discussion no great emphasis was laid on the validity of the reconciliation. It is my best recollection that he kept no record of marks based on daily recitations."

Another member of the same class, Dean Albert J. Harno, of the Law School of the University of Indiana, writes the following:[3]

"I was a senior in the Yale Law School when William Howard Taft came there and I had the privilege of being one of the first students in his class in Constitutional Law. Naturally the experience of taking work under a man who had so recently been President of the United States made a deep impression on me.

"Mr. Taft had many calls on his time but we found him an approachable and congenial individual. Although I have sat under more stimulating teachers than he, his instruction was good and his classes were exceedingly interesting. Often in the midst of a discussion of constitutional principles, he would suddenly begin to chuckle and tell us of an experience he had had with some phase of the case before us, or, better still, relate some personal experience he had had with the judge or the attorneys in the case. We used, as I recall it, Thayer's *Cases on Constitutional Law*, a big book. But Mr. Taft did not limit himself to it. He resorted

3. Harno to Hicks, April 10, 1940.

# Professor in Yale Law School

most freely and at times with utter abandon, I thought, to the citation of cases for outside reading. What is more, he held us responsible for these cases in class recitation. Now it must be said that cases in constitutional law in the original reports often run to considerable length. I remember one weekend, after I had read opinions until I was sure I was about to lose my eyesight and still was not making much headway, I made a count of the pages involved and found he had asked us to read cases covering 604 pages.

"In his teaching he did not go beyond the orthodox concepts of constitutional law, and his analyses were not penetrating. At this distance my most vivid recollection of him is of his abundant personality. I feel it now; it filled the classroom and dwarfed all else by way of comparison. Yes, indeed, I count it as an experience to have sat in his classes."

That Taft was careless in estimating the amount of work that a student could do in a fixed period of time is emphasized by the comment of one of his colleagues, Professor Edmund M. Morgan, now of the Harvard Law School, who writes[4] that "his examinations in Constitutional Law were the talk of the School. Ordinarily he put no questions which could not be answered out of the cases in the casebook, but he put them at some length so that he felt obliged to allow the students the entire day to answer the questions, although the regulation time was four hours."

William B. Gumbart, LL.B. 1915, in a letter of July 16, 1940, writes the following:

"I had already taken Constitutional Law when Taft came to the Law School, but I used to attend the

4. Morgan to Hicks, April 3, 1940.

classes as an auditor, not because I wanted to hear
him on Constitutional Law, but because of the intense
interest of the stories he had to tell of his career as
lawyer, Judge, Governor of the Philippines, Cabinet
officer, and President.

"One of the things I remember is that one day he
was telling us of his interest in the Insular cases.
While he was Governor of the Philippines, he had
worked on the brief, although he did not appear as
counsel in the cases. He went on to tell how Justice
Edward D. White had agreed with his, Taft's, position, dissenting in one case and writing the majority
opinion in another. The dissent undoubtedly was that
in the case of DeLima v. Bidwell, 182 U.S. 1. The dissent, beginning on page 200, was written by McKenna,
with Shiras and White joining in the dissent. The other
case was probably that of United States v. Heinszen
Co., 206 U.S. 370, in which White delivered the
opinion of the Court which upheld the statute, which
I believe Taft had been instrumental in having Congress pass. Having told of White's concurrence with
his own views, Taft then, with his characteristic
chuckle, said, 'and when I was President, Mr. White
became Chief Justice.' This is an interesting sidelight
on the appointment of White.

"In connection with the question in the Insular
cases of whether the Constitution follows the flag, according to Pringle's *The Life and Times of William
Howard Taft*, Taft wrote to Judge Harlan as follows:

"I do not know who it is that said so, but it amused
me very much when I heard it, that the position of
the court was in this wise: that four of the judges
said the Constitution did follow the flag, that four of

them said it did not . . . and one said, 'it sometimes follows the flag and sometimes does not, and I will tell you when it does and when it does not' (p. 208).

"My recollection of the way Taft told the story is: 'Some of the judges say she do, and some say she don't, but I'm the boy to tell you when she do and when she don't.' "

Another sidelight is thrown on these same cases by Professor Edwin Borchard who recalls[5] that at a Law Faculty meeting Taft said to him that he thought one of the things which attracted President Theodore Roosevelt to Taft was the latter's suggestion of a way to overcome the effect of the decision of the Supreme Court[6] holding invalid certain tariff duties illegally imposed on imports into the Philippine Islands between 1899 and 1902. "It was feared," wrote Professor Borchard, "that the Federal government might have to refund millions in improperly collected taxes. Mr. Taft at a Cabinet meeting suggested that a simple way to overcome the defects of the original statutes was to pass a new act ratifying the collection of the tariff duties illegally imposed and curing the defect. President Roosevelt thought this a fine suggestion, and said it should at once be tried out. Thereupon an Act of June 30, 1906 (34 St. at L. 636), was passed, and the Supreme Court duly sustained it as constitutional in United States v. Heinszen. Mr. Taft maintained that the successful outcome of this suit endeared him to President Roosevelt, and probably had much to do with Roosevelt's selection of him as his successor in 1908."

5. Borchard to Hicks, June 12, 1940.
6. Warner, Barnes and Co. v. United States, 197 U.S. 419 (1905).

# William Howard Taft

The preceding excerpts from letters of students relate to the year 1913–14, the first of Taft's teaching. Concerning the class in the third year thereafter, 1915–16, William M. Gager, LL.B. 1916, says:[7]

"Professor Taft taught me such little Constitutional Law as I know. I also for several years marked his course in Constitutional Law given to the academic senior class. I considered him a good teacher, particularly in the sense that he brought clearly to the understanding of the student the fact that law is a matter of human experience and growth and not an abstract and purely scientific study. In the field of Constitutional Law I think this was of particular benefit in that it brought home that by the process of interpretation the Constitution was constantly being adapted to new situations not within the knowledge or prevision of the framers of the Constitution, thus retaining a semblance of permanency together with a constant changing in application fitting the needs of the immediate times.

"I emphasize this point in his teaching rather than the mere mechanical teaching of existing law because it differentiates him from that type of teacher who has a thorough knowledge of his subject but an entire lack of knowledge of the philosophy in back of the law."

Sidney W. Davidson, LL.B. 1918, elected his course in the year 1917–18. Of the class in that year he writes:[8]

"The class consisted of less than a dozen students. All of us became closely acquainted with him in the classroom.

"He conducted his classes methodically. He called

7. Gager to Hicks, May 20, 1940.
8. Davidson to Hicks, October 14, 1940.

on each student in turn to recite the cases included in the assignment. He was intent upon covering a fixed number of cases each day. I recall one occasion when he failed to appear in the classroom on time. After waiting nearly half an hour some of the students left, but two or three of us lingered on the front steps of Hendrie Hall. Professor Taft was then seen hurrying across the Green. He greeted us on the steps genially and said: 'Come along: let's cover the cases assigned for today even though there are only a few of us here to recite them.' The assignment was recited accordingly.

"Professor Taft did not conform to the technique of other professors in the Law School and made slight attempt to coördinate his teaching with that of his colleagues. Early in the course he was embarrassed by questions put by students which were based upon Professor Hohfeld's system of legal analysis which had first been published in 1913 in 23 *Yale Law Journal*, 16. That system was a foundation for much of the teaching in the Law School and most of the professors applied the Hohfeld analysis rigidly in their courses. During the fall term it developed from statements which Professor Taft frankly made in class that while he had heard of Professor Hohfeld's article, he had never read it, but that he hoped to read it some day.

"After a routine recital of the assigned cases, a student would occasionally ask Professor Taft to reconcile the opinion in one case with opinions in other cases which seemed *contra*. Professor Taft rarely took an interest in discussing conflicting legal theories and often dodged questions of that character by chuckling and telling a story. Throughout the course he related abundant personal incidents concerning judges, counsel and litigants involved in the assigned cases. They were drawn from his own broad experience and that of his father. I believe that Mr. Taft's professorship was of great benefit to the Law School in view of his eminence and the rare experience afforded to his students to become closely acquainted with one of the great personalities of his time."

One of the extraneous things that occasionally gave special interest to Taft's law classes was the presence of distinguished visitors. For example, when Nicholas Longworth came to New Haven to make a campaign speech, he said he wanted to hear Taft lecture, and Edward A. Harriman took him to the classroom. On his return from long lecture trips in connection with American preparations for World War I, he would tell of his experiences, and answer questions about them. Sidney W. Davidson recalls that on Taft's return from a tour of army camps, speaking to draftees, he was asked by the class whether he had had a successful trip. "Yes," he replied. "I always consider any speech to be successful if more of the audience stay than leave during the course of the speech. During my speeches to draftees, not a single man left." He delighted fraternity groups by speaking at their dinners, where he interspersed his serious remarks with humorous stories. Edward A. Harriman, a Harvard graduate who was a lecturer in the Yale Law School in 1915–16, recalls[9] an example of Taft's adroitness in applying his remarks to the occasion. At a Corbey Court dinner, Harriman was introduced as a Harvard man. Taft spoke directly after Harriman. He said he was glad

9. Harriman to Hicks, May 19, 1940.

that a Harvard man was present, although the fact reminded him of a story of an Irishman who was tried for murder in Tipperary. "It seems," said Taft, "that there was a fair in Tipperary, and that the prisoner at the bar, in a quarrel, had hit a man with a blackthorn stick, and killed him, because the deceased had what is known as a paper skull, so thin that the blow from the blackthorn crushed it. The jury brought in a verdict of guilty, and the judge asked the prisoner if he had anything to say why sentence of death should not be pronounced upon him. 'My Lord,' said the prisoner, 'I would like to ask one question.' 'Very well,' said the judge, 'if it is a proper question, you may ask it.' 'My Lord,' said the prisoner, 'all I want to ask is this: What the divvle was a man with a skull like that doin' in Tipperary?' "

A thing that several students recall with pleasure is Taft's ability to call them by name when they happened to meet him years after they had been in his classes, and when Taft had become Chief Justice of the United States.

More important than any of the foregoing as an indication of the place that Taft filled in the life of the Law School is the story of his relations with the Law Faculty. Dean Rogers' desire that he give courses in the Law School has already been noted.[10] After the connection had been established, Rogers prepared a longer statement[11] in which he expressed the gratification of the Law Faculty, that Taft was a colleague. After recalling the circumstances under which other great Americans had turned to teaching on their re-

10. Chapter I.
11. *Yale Daily News*, April 16, 1913.

tirement from public life—Kent at Columbia, Benjamin Harrison at Leland Stanford, Lee at Washington and Lee University, Story at Harvard, Cleveland at Princeton—he concluded by saying: "It is not only that Mr. Taft has been President of the United States, but that he is recognized generally as a man who would have made an admirable Chief Justice of the Supreme Court of the United States. The men who are preparing for the practice of the law will be most fortunate to have the benefit of his instruction, and to be brought into personal relations with so great a teacher and so inspiring a personality." Others thought then, and retained the belief many years afterward, that he would be good for the school, even if he were not technically a great teacher. This was the opinion of the late George D. Watrous, who said five years ago,[12] "I have always felt that the personality of a law teacher was more important to the students than any formal teaching. If a teacher made the student feel that he was the kind of man he, the student, would like to be, he had done a good job. I used to say in substance that if Mr. Taft did no more than smile upon his students, chuckle now and then, and tell them some appropriate legal anecdotes, it would justify his appointment."

The Law Faculty into which Taft came in 1913 consisted of thirteen members. The full-time teachers were Dean Rogers, John Wurts, Ralph W. Gifford, Arthur L. Corbin, John W. Edgerton, and Charles P. Sherman. The part-time members were Samuel O. Prentice, Edwin B. Gager, John K. Beach, George D. Watrous, George E. Beers, Gordon E. Sherman, and

12. Watrous to Hicks, March 29, 1940.

# Professor in Yale Law School

Simeon E. Baldwin. Taft enjoyed his relations with these men. Wurts was a college classmate. In spite of the fact that his sentimental attachments were with the College, it is the opinion of Professor Corbin that he felt more at home in the Law School. This is understandable because he had already been a law teacher, and a law dean, and knew the problems of law school administration. He could talk with his colleagues the language of lawyers, and he found that law students were more serious in their attitude toward their studies than college students usually were toward their courses. The approach toward the subject matter was professional, and this was a satisfaction to him.

The appointment of Taft to teach part-time did not accord with one of the objectives then being sought in the Law School. In his annual report for 1911–12, Dean Rogers had said that "instruction is now given almost exclusively by resident professors who devote their entire time to the work of the School and who are withdrawn from the active practice of the law."[13] This plan had the hearty approval of Thomas W. Swan, who succeeded Rogers as Dean in 1916, and steady progress was to be made under him toward the goal of having most of the teaching done by full-time professors. That he was far from being unappreciative of work done by part-time teachers, including Taft, appears from the following excerpt from his annual report of 1916–17:

"The validity of the principle that the main work of law teaching should be in the hands of men who devote themselves exclusively to instruction has been

13. Hicks, F. C., *Yale Law School: 1895–1915*, Yale Law Library Publications, No. 7, p. 45.

generally recognized in the leading universities and was strongly emphasized in Dean Rogers' report for last year. While the bulk of the teaching work should be in the hands of full-time professors, it is realized also that students receive great inspiration from contact with distinguished judges and lawyers in active practice. The School is fortunate in having on its Faculty men of this type and in being able to retain for next year, as in the years past, the valued services of ex-Governor Baldwin, ex-President Taft, Judge Henry Wade Rogers, Judge Edwin B. Gager, and Judge John K. Beach."

There is no evidence that the resident professors who were attached to the Law School when Taft came, or those who joined the Faculty in later years, were unfavorably disposed to his retention on the Faculty. This is an important commentary on him, because these professors are the men who in that period had most to do with the signal progress made by the school. The men specially referred to are Arthur L. Corbin, John W. Edgerton, and Ralph W. Gifford, who were on hand to greet him when he came; and the following who joined the Faculty in later years as indicated by the dates which follow their names: Wesley N. Hohfeld (1914–15), Dean Swan and Walter W. Cook (1916–17); Edwin Borchard, Ernest G. Lorenzen, and Edmund M. Morgan, all of whom came in 1917–18; and 1919–20, Charles E. Clark, Karl N. Llewellyn, and Edward S. Thurston.

They found him always on the side of higher standards for the school. At the same time he was, as Professor Borchard says,[14] "exceedingly modest in his at-

14. Borchard to Hicks, June 12, 1940.

titude as a teacher of both of his subjects [Constitutional Law and International Law]. While he never professed to be a scholar, he nevertheless had an excellent control at least of Constitutional Law. He often said that he knew nothing of international law, but actually his practical experience had taught him a great deal." The fact that he was a member of the Law School Faculty, but not of the smaller number of full-time professors who constituted its Governing Board, had no significance as regards the attitude of the law professors toward him. The stipulation in the resolution of the Prudential Committee of March 1, 1913,[15] "had no substantial effect on his influence in the school for the reason that at that period the affairs of the school were in all important respects determined at monthly meetings of the Faculty."[16] He was a respected, working member of the Faculty, who had no desire to be Dean. Professor Corbin tells how he received the suggestion when in 1913 it was proposed that he succeed Dean Rogers: "At the Faculty meeting when he was first notified, he at once declined the offer. Chuckling in his inimitable way, he said in almost these words: 'You don't want a man like me for Dean. You need a young man who will make it his career, and who must succeed by making the Law School succeed. In my younger days, I was myself dean of a law school for a few years, and I know the requirements.' "

He attended Faculty meetings with considerable regularity, even after the novelty of being a professor had worn off. The records show, for example, that he

15. See Chapter I.
16. Statement of Professor Arthur L. Corbin, April 20, 1940.

attended meetings on October 9, 16, 30, and November 13, 20, 27, 1917; on January 8, 15, April 9, 23, 1918; and on December 2, 1919. He attended many of the weekly Faculty luncheons which Dean Swan started. When business was being transacted "he was an alert and interested participant," says Professor Corbin, "expressing frank opinions when appealed to, but always professing to be less wise than others." He added greatly to the goodfellowship of the weekly gatherings. Professor Thurston said on this point that "he was about the most genial man I have ever known. To hear him tell a funny story, which he often did at our Faculty luncheons, was a treat. He often sat next to Judge Beach, who called him Bill. Beach was very small and Taft was enormous. The contrast was striking to one sitting opposite to them, as I usually did."[17] Beach was graduated from Yale in 1877, one year before Taft. One of the first to invite Taft to play golf in New Haven, in 1913, was Beach. It must have been a sight to behold when the birdlike Beach walked across the Green with the ponderous Taft.

It is not surprising that there is a difference of opinion among former students on the question whether Taft approved of the "case method" of instruction. This is because he did not in his own classes give a convincing demonstration of this method, of which, in theory, and as successfully applied by others, he heartily approved. Twelve years before he came to Yale he had adopted the method for use in the Cincinnati Law School of which he was Dean. In the meantime, he said that he had observed that students

17. Thurston to Hicks, June 8, 1940.

trained by this method were better prepared for practice than were those who came from schools which used another method. He undoubtedly thought that he was using the case method in his Yale Law School classes. He used casebooks instead of textbooks, and he required students to discuss cases in class; but before long, in each session, he involuntarily began his own exposition of the cases in what amounted to a discursive, informative, and often humorous lecture. The contrast between his classroom technique and that of some of the younger members of the Faculty must have been, in this respect, very noticeable to students. But he was in fact a strong supporter of the progressive plans of these younger professors, under the leadership of Professor Corbin, not only as to methods of instruction, but also as to other matters. The situation is summed up in the following statement prepared by Professor Corbin:

"Before Mr. Taft's arrival here, the faculty had already put the case system in full operation. In his own course, Mr. Taft used Thayer's Cases for two years, and thereafter used Wambaugh's Cases. It was never suggested that he had any question that the case system was best. The catalogue next preceding Mr. Taft's election to the Faculty shows that a case book was used in every course except Code Pleading and a few short lecture courses. The old required course in Elementary Law (condensed Blackstone) was abolished. Requirements for admission to the school as a student were graduation from an approved college or membership in the senior class of Yale College. The Law Faculty was still in part composed of judges and practicing lawyers; but they were of advanced years, and the policy of building a faculty of full-time professional teachers was already accepted.

"The adoption of these three important changes in policy—case system, entrance requirements, full-time professors—had never created any open rupture; but the student body was greatly reduced in number, and funds for obtaining and holding teachers of established reputation were lacking. There were some expressions of dissatisfaction among alumni; and some of the older members of the Faculty had doubts. The prompt and openly expressed approval of all these policies by Mr. Taft was of very great assistance to the younger members of the Faculty. After his arrival, there was never anything but whole-hearted support in the Faculty for our ambitious and progressive programme. To the older men who had once held strongly opposing views, the fact that ex-President Taft approved was accepted as convincing evidence. It must be remembered, however, that they had themselves accepted the new programme before Mr. Taft's arrival. To the younger men who had been ardent instigators of the programme, Mr. Taft's support gave immense satisfaction and assured confidence. He exactly filled their need by adding the ponderous weight of his personality, his prestige with Yale men, and his great judicial and administrative experience."[18]

On these important matters of policy, there is no doubt where Taft stood. In his personal conduct which might affect the successful operation of the school, and make difficulties for its administrative head, he was

18. For an account of the adoption of these new policies see Hicks, F. C., *Yale Law School: 1895–1915*, Yale Law Library Publications, No. 7.

thoughtful and unassuming. Dean Swan writes of these characteristics as follows:[19] "He was conscientious about keeping his class appointments,[20] and whenever this was impossible, he was most punctilious to call at the Dean's office, ask my permission, and explain that the recitation would be made up on a later day. It seemed almost ludicrous for an ex-President to ask a neophyte dean for leave to cut classes. He must have known, of course, that the request would never be denied. I suppose the fact that Mr. Taft had himself been a law school dean made him particularly careful to observe the formality of reporting an intended absence from classes."

19. Swan to Hicks, October 7, 1943.
20. He might be late, but he usually got there.

# V

## Formal Academic Lectures

Among Taft's activities outside of the classroom, not the least important were the several series of lectures which he gave at the invitation of academic institutions, including Yale. These lectures are the formal expression of his thought on subjects of public interest, embodying the ideas which he deemed to be fundamental to the American way of living, and which, as a professor, he was anxious to impress upon audiences made up largely of students and instructors throughout the country.

Twice before becoming a Yale professor, while he was Secretary of War, he had given such lectures. The first was on June 26, 1905, an address to the graduating class of the Yale Law School, on the Administration of Criminal Law. This was printed in the *Yale Law Journal*, and in pamphlet form, by the school, and later in Taft's *Present Day Problems, A Collection of Addresses Delivered on Various Occasions*.[1] It was initially an argument that it would be inadvisable to try to impose American criminal law procedure, particularly the jury system, upon the Philippine Islands and Puerto Rico. From this beginning it proceeded to an examination of the operation of criminal law in the United States, in comparison with the actual operation of similar rules in England. It reached a conclusion which, when published, produced a sensation. Said he, "I grieve for my country to say that the administration of the criminal law in all the States of the Union (there may

1. New York, Dodd, Mead & Co., 1908, pp. 333-335.

be one or two exceptions) is a disgrace to our civilization."

Taft's second appearance at Yale as an academic lecturer was in 1906, when he was the William E. Dodge lecturer on the foundation to provide lectures on the general topic "Responsibilities of Citizenship." Other lecturers on this foundation before 1906 had been Mr. Justice David J. Brewer, Bishop Henry Codman Potter, and President Arthur T. Hadley. Among those who followed Taft in subsequent years were Elihu Root, James Bryce, Charles Evans Hughes, Lyman Abbott, and Simeon E. Baldwin. Taft's lectures, given on four successive nights, were published in 1906 for the Yale University Press by Charles Scribner's Sons, with the title *Four Aspects of Civic Duty*. The book was reprinted in 1916 and again in 1918 by the Yale University Press. The four aspects discussed were chosen out of Taft's own experience. He viewed the duties of citizenship from the standpoint, first, of a recent graduate of a university, second, of a judge on the bench, third, of a colonial administrator, and fourth, of a national executive.

These are optimistic lectures, easy to read, given by a man who felt sure of himself, and who was confident that our system of government was essentially good, and that despite errors and imperfections, all would work out for the best. He reiterated his criticisms of our administration of criminal law, but was sure that if educated people would not avoid service on juries, if they would take an active part in politics, and in the choice of judges, the system would be found to be workable. His advice to college men to enter politics was a favorite theme with him, which he reverted to

throughout the years. An example is his address[2] in
1928, two years before his death, at a Yale alumni
luncheon on the occasion of the fiftieth reunion of his
class of 1878. He urged Yale graduates to engage in
local politics and work up through the ranks to positions of influence.

In these Dodge Lectures he condemned socialism,
coupled the right of personal liberty with the right of
property, defended capital, but supported the anti-
trust law, and thought that corporations must be re-
strained from the misuse of their powers. He was
against muckraking, contrasted freedom of the press
and the duty of citizens not to criticize public servants
unjustly, thought that the "discipline of a fear of
publicity" was good for executives, and warned that
national interests are sometimes opposed to local interests, so that "popular government must be a series
of compromises."

The first lectures that he gave at Yale, in May,
1913, after he became a professor, have already been
referred to. They discussed "Questions of Modern
Government." His text for these lectures was the preamble of the Constitution of the United States. Start-
ing with the phrase "We, the people of the United
States," he extolled the virtues of representative
government as a necessary part of the democratic system applied to large democracies, and he condemned
as dangerous the current agitation for the initiative,
referendum, and recall. The phrase "to form a more
perfect Union" gave him opportunity to discuss the
relation of States' rights to Federal powers. Three lectures were devoted to the phrase "to establish justice,"

2. See Chapter IX.

with emphasis on the selection and tenure of judges, and further denunciation of the proposed recall of judges and decisions which he said would be an unwarranted method of nullifying judge-made law. "To insure domestic tranquillity, provide for the common defense" was developed into a discussion of war and peace under the Constitution, the status of the army and the navy, and settlement of international controversies through diplomatic negotiations and by arbitration.

In May, 1914, Taft delivered five lectures on the Edward D. Page Foundation before the seniors of the Sheffield Scientific School at Yale University. This Foundation was established to promote "the ethical side of business life, including the morals and ethics of public service." The lectures were given in Room 31, North Sheffield Hall, at 5 P.M. on successive Tuesdays, the last being delivered on May 26. Taft chose as his subject "Ethics in Service," and the lectures were published with that title, in October, 1915, by the Yale University Press. The subjects of his five lectures are: "History of the Profession of Law," "Legal Ethics," "The Executive Power," "The Signs of the Times," and "More Signs of the Times."

The first two lectures were of the traditional legal sort, and might have been given by any older lawyer of standing. In the other three, however, Taft dealt with matters which he could illustrate from recent personal experiences, and with current events upon which he had strong convictions touched with emotion. The lecture on "The Executive Power" was the forerunner of a series of lectures on the same subject which will presently be discussed; and the two on "Signs of the Times" were, with modifications, to serve him again and again as vehicles for pointing out dangers which he thought ought to be avoided. He was satirical about "reformers-for-politics-only" and "muckraking," came out strongly against his *bête noire*, the initiative, referendum, and recall, defended representative government which he said, if properly conducted, made it needless to give "more democracy to supply the present defects of our existing democracy," and on the whole was optimistic about the future.

"We are living," he said, "at a time when political and social conditions are a bit chaotic, and it is a little difficult to distinguish between the symptoms that are ephemeral and those which are permanent. What we must do is try to make things better and to save from the past the things which are good. It is often true that a movement that is excessive and destructive in one way, ends by being the basis of great progress after reaction from its excesses has left what is valuable in it."

Taft's talks about his experiences while President of the United States were always in demand. When speaking to private audiences, for example, the members of the Graduates Club of New Haven, his off-the-record remarks were amusing and very frank. Even in his formal lectures on this subject he spoke with considerable freedom so that his listeners felt that they were getting inside information, and were being taken into the confidence of the former Chief Magistrate. That was the impression that they got from the Page Lecture on "The Executive Power," already referred to, given at the Sheffield Scientific School. Taft sensed this interest, and responded to the desire expressed in many quarters that he go into the subject more at length. The result was a series of three lectures which he gave on four occasions, and which were published by two different institutions. In their final form these lectures are recognized as of permanent value, and undoubtedly they were the most successful of his academic addresses. They had a wide popular appeal. They were given first at the University of Chicago, November 18–20, 1914; second at the University of Virginia, January, 1915; third at the University of Toronto, February, 1915; and finally at Columbia University, October, 1915.

Those given at the University of Virginia were on the Barbour-Page Foundation, established by Mrs. Thomas Nelson Page, and they were published in April, 1916, by Charles Scribner's Sons with the title *The Presidency; Its Duties, Its Powers, Its Opportunities and Its Limitations*. The enthusiastic reception of these lectures may be seen in the following excerpt quoted from *College Topics* by the *Yale Daily News*, February 5, 1915:

"*A Tribute to Professor Taft.* Never since the Barbour-Page Lectures have featured the purely university work at Virginia have we been better entertained than by the lectures of Mr. Taft. His amiable manners, thorough and intimate acquaintance with his subject, his entire unaffectedness and good humor, have won him many hundreds of new friends during his stay here. We have had many notable personages, and many fine scholars among former Barbour-Page lecturers, but we venture to say that none of them has delivered lectures which have had the value as human documents which

Mr. Taft's possessed. They were scholarly without pedantry, humorous without boisterousness or any hint of bad taste, and instructive without tediousness.

"Mr. Taft's greatest contribution in these lectures was his manner of illustrating his views of the Presidential powers with entertaining reminiscences of events of his own administration. There are scores of people who know quite as much as Mr. Taft about the theory of the executive powers, but his treatment of the subject as a personal one has lifted it above the level of the theoretical into the realm of living history. We hope that these addresses will shortly be published, either in their present, or in more amplified form, for the benefit of people everywhere. They contain quite the most interesting treatment of the subject with which we are familiar and throw much light on an administration which is of much importance in American history, coming as it did at a time when many great forces were in operation to altogether change the tenor of the American political situation."

How Taft won his audience is illustrated by his opening remarks, "I claim no special learning from the books as to the presidency," he said, "but I can bring practical experience that the necessary paucity in living ex-Presidents makes somewhat exceptional. Mr. Squeers, in explaining to Nicholas Nickleby the system of vocational and practical study pursued at Dotheboys Hall, required the boy first to spell 'winders' and then to go and clean 'winders,' in order that the subject might be well fixed in his mind. I have merely reversed the process, and, having tried to clean the 'winders,' I am here to make some effort correctly to spell the word."

# Formal Academic Lectures

In the preparation of these lectures, Taft did not set up a formal outline to be rigidly followed, but apparently let one thought suggest another as he went along. The result must have been that the listeners were carried along with the speaker much as is the case in an interesting conversation dominated by one personality. Roughly speaking, the argument deals with the powers of the President as legislator (veto power), his executive powers as defined by the Constitution, his duties in the execution of laws passed by Congress (including their interpretation as a preliminary to action), his relation to foreign affairs, and the powers which he sometimes feels obliged to exercise, for the general welfare, in times of emergency.

Some of the opinions incidentally expressed are that it might have been better to elect the President for a term of seven years, with no reëlection; that members of the Cabinet, which is not a Constitutional body, ought to be allowed access to the floor of each House for the purpose of advocating and explaining proposed legislation; that the President's veto power should be exercised not only when he thinks an act is unconstitutional, but also when he questions the expediency or the wisdom of approving it (since the President more truly represents the whole country than does the majority in either House); that Federal activities should not be extended at the expense of States rights, but nevertheless the growth of Federal administrative agencies is inevitable, in order to get things done; that the President's power of appointing public officers carries with it the power of removal (without the consent of the Senate); that only important positions should be filled by presidential appointment, the others being put under a classified service; that "advice and consent" of the Senate means in practice advice and consent of the leaders of the dominant party in the Senate at the time; and that the President's Constitutional powers are in fact much more limited than is ordinarily supposed.

These same lectures were given by Mr. Taft in October, 1915, at Columbia University, on the George Blumenthal Foundation, in the Horace Mann auditorium. Harlan Fiske Stone, then Dean of the Columbia University Law School, and now Chief Justice of the Supreme Court of the United States, presided. They were published in May, 1916, by the Columbia University Press, and were reprinted in January, 1925, with an introduction by Nicholas Murray Butler.

In the printed Blumenthal Lectures, the book is divided into six chapters in order to mark more formally the divisions of the subject, but this only serves to accentuate the rather casual character of the outline. The points are a little more fully stated and they are supported by more material of a historical character. To his discussion of President Jefferson's action in the New Orleans Batture cases, in which was involved the question whether the President had exceeded his Constitutional powers, he added a favorable account of the career of Edward Livingston, Jefferson's opponent in the argument. On this same subject, assumption of powers not specifically given to the President by the Constitution, both the Barbour-Page and the Blumenthal Lectures quote Theodore Roosevelt's views expressed in his *Notes for a Possible Autobiography*. In the Blumenthal Lectures (pp. 143–144), Taft added the following, which must have amused his audience, and which is a good example of the type of humor for which he was famous:

"I may add that Mr. Roosevelt, by way of illustrating his meaning as to the differing usefulness of Presidents, divides the Presidents into two classes, and designates them as 'Lincoln Presidents' and 'Buchanan Presidents.' In order more fully to illustrate his division of Presidents on their merits, he places himself in in the Lincoln class of Presidents, and me in the Buchanan class. The identification of Mr. Roosevelt with Mr. Lincoln might otherwise have escaped notice, because there are many differences between the two, presumably superficial, which would give the impartial student of history a different impression. It suggests a story which a friend of mine told of his little daughter Mary. As he came walking home after a business day, she ran out from the house to greet him, all aglow with the importance of what she wished to tell him. She said, 'Papa, I am the best scholar in the class.' The father's heart throbbed with pleasure as he inquired, 'Why, Mary, you surprise me. When did the teacher tell you? This afternoon?' 'Oh, no,' Mary's reply was, 'the teacher didn't tell me—I just noticed it myself.' "

While on leave in 1921, the year in which he became Chief Justice, Taft delivered two lectures which were published. The first was given on April 30, 1921, in Town Hall, New York City, on the foundation established in New York University by James Stokes. The title is *Representative Government in the United States.*[2] The second was delivered at the University of Rochester, in the series established by James Goold Cutler. It was published by the Yale University Press

2. New York University Press, 1921.

in 1922, with the title, *Liberty under Law: an Interpretation of the Principles of Our Constitutional Government*. Both of these lectures are dignified and conservative, covering no new ground, but reiterating views expressed in part on many other occasions. The passing years had not caused him to change his mind, or to despair of success under the existing frame of government.

These several series of lectures, all of which survived in print, by no means represent all of his appearances as lecturer in institutions of learning. He lectured also at Boston University Law School, University of Minnesota Law School and Albany Law School; and at Amherst, Bryn Mawr, Harvard, Smith, Vassar, and Wesleyan University. And in addition, whenever he visited a college town for any purpose, he was pressed into service for impromptu addresses at chapel, in assembly rooms, and at luncheons and banquets. Thus one prearranged address, perhaps to a Chamber of Commerce, might involve one or two other brief talks to hastily assembled academic audiences.

# VI

## Other Lectures and Addresses

For most of the academic addresses already described, Taft was probably recompensed in accordance with the provisions of the foundations under which they were given. He was paid substantial fees also for many other addresses given outside of New Haven. Pringle says (p. 856) that he received fees "ranging from $150 to as high as $1,000—with $400 as a probable average," and that Taft's secretary, Wendell W. Mischler, became "a one-man lecture bureau." There is nothing inaccurate about these statements, but they should not be allowed to convey the impression that Taft gave public addresses only when he was paid for them. Quite the contrary is the case, as will presently be shown.

It was understood when Taft came to Yale that he would devote much of his time to public matters and addresses, and his schedule of College and Law School classes was arranged with this in mind. The list of speaking engagements that I have compiled shows that at first many of his public appearances were of a kind for which no compensation could be expected. As the demand increased and as the requests came from points more and more distant, it obviously was necessary to systematize his speaking schedule, and to set up a scale of fees. With engagements coming thick and fast, it was essential to be prepared in advance. He had his "Questions of Modern Government" Lectures, his Page Lectures, and his expanded lectures on the presidency; but these were not enough. Therefore, he drew up a list of subjects on which he could speak, and composed them in outline whenever he had time.

Mr. Mischler writes that "we got out a list of thirty subjects on which he would lecture, such as the Duties of Citizenship, the Initiative and Referendum, Judicial Recall, etc. To anyone making application to have Mr. Taft lecture, one of these lists would be sent and the party could make his choice of subject. . . . I could book him as far as Iowa, to lecture there on a Saturday evening, for then he could take the midnight train out of there on a Saturday night, and get back to New Haven in ample time for his first lecture on Monday."[1]

It is a remarkable fact that Taft had no research assistants to help him in preparing his addresses and articles at any time when he was in New Haven. He did all the work himself, working very rapidly.

In the White House he had had a large collection of books. When he left Washington in 1913, he had the books shipped to New Haven, where they were put in storage. After awhile, he shipped them back to Washington to be placed in the rooms that had been assigned to him in the Congressional Library. In his office in the Hotel Taft,[2] he had some law books which he used in preparing his lectures on Constitutional Law. These books were kept in good physical condition by an assistant from the Yale Law Library. Any other books that he needed were borrowed from the libraries of the University.

The list of books that he borrowed from the main library of the University has been preserved. The use

1. Mischler to Hicks, May 21, 1940.
2. For some unknown reason, he never had an office on the University campus.

to which he put these books is plainly seen by comparing their subjects with the subjects of his addresses and writings. For example, as he expanded his lectures on the presidency, he progressively went further into the works of President Jefferson, and of Edward Livingston, reading also their biographies, and finally borrowing from the Law Library the *American Law Journal*, 1814, which contains the documents in the Batture cases, already referred to.[3] Sometimes his requests involved physical difficulties for the library staff. Once he asked to have the *Encyclopedia Britanica* sent to his office. There was only one set in the library, and so the volumes were brought to him by messengers, who waited while he consulted the articles in which he was interested.

Included among his borrowings were many periodicals, such as issues of the *Arena*, the *Independent*, the *Outlook*, the *Yale Review*, the *Review of Reviews*, *World's Work*, the *New England Magazine*, the *Annual Register*, the *International Journal of Ethics*, the *Spectator*, *Political Science Quarterly*, *American Philosophical Society Proceedings*, and the *American Journal of International Law*. The subjects of the books borrowed ranged from history to philosophy, to ethics, to religion, with a preponderance of works on political science, politics, protection, reciprocity, international law, the Concert of Europe, arbitration and world organization.

Occasionally he went to the library to look over the new books, and he was friendly in his relations with the library staff.

Taft was kept busy preparing new addresses adapted

3. Chapter V.

to particular occasions, or suggested by current events. Most of them were fully composed. Sometimes he read to his audiences from a typed copy, but often he had the draft before him only to serve as an outline while he spoke extemporaneously or from memory.

He dictated each lecture or article to Mr. Mischler, and after the original was handed to him, he would complete it in two drafts. He pushed himself very hard, but never seemed to become irritated or nervously overwrought. Mischler was at work nearly every night in the four-room office on the sixth floor of the Hotel Taft. Between the two men there was a fine understanding. Taft described his secretary as "my dear friend and indispensable co-worker, a model of accuracy, foresight, intelligence and loyalty, without whose aid I could not do half the work I do." Mischler began work with Taft when the latter became Secretary of War in February, 1904. When Taft was nominated for the presidency, Mischler resigned his position in the War Department, in order to accompany the candidate on his campaign tours, and report his speeches stenographically. After the election he became one of the President's two assistant secretaries. After the defeat of 1912, Mischler came to New Haven as Taft's secretary, and he was retained as secretary to the Chief Justice. With Mr. Taft he visited every state in the Union, went to Panama five times, to Cuba and Puerto Rico, and spent sixteen summers at the Taft summer home in Murray Bay, Quebec. After the death of Chief Justice Taft, Mr. Mischler became secretary to Chief Justice Hughes, and later secretary to Mr. Hughes in private life.

Of the several hundred speeches that Taft delivered

outside of New Haven, only a surmise can be made whether many of them were or were not on a fee basis. Presumably those given to Chambers of Commerce, commercial clubs, bankers' clubs, associations of manufacturers, business men's clubs, women's clubs, and press clubs, were recompensed. Those which in all probability were not paid for are much more numerous. They may roughly be divided into the following groups: speeches before Yale alumni associations; legal speeches before bar associations and legislatures (he was president of the American Bar Association in 1913); addresses before churches, charitable organizations and associations of teachers; speeches at dedication ceremonies, and at national expositions; political speeches; Red Cross and Liberty Loan speeches; and peace and League of Nations speeches.

As time went on, the subjects of his addresses became more and more often determined by current events. He spoke on the Mexican situation in 1914; on labor, on prohibition, and on woman's suffrage. The European war brought out many speeches on neutrality, the rights of neutrals, the Monroe Doctrine, and preparedness for defense. He was one of the most successful Liberty and Victory Loan speakers, and he traveled 8,000 miles in January and February, 1918, speaking in army camps. The National War Council of the Young Men's Christian Association bore all expenses of this trip. Another long tour was in October, 1916, when he spoke every night except Sunday in support of the presidential candidacy of Charles E. Hughes.

All of these together were as little or nothing compared to his continuous interest and activity on the subject of peace, a world court, international adjustment after the war, and a League of Nations.

In the winter of 1913–14, he delivered four lectures before the New York Peace Society. They were published in *The Independent*, and in book form as *The United States and Peace*.[4] The titles of the lectures were (1) "The Monroe Doctrine: Its Limitations and Implications"; (2) "Shall the Federal Government Protect Aliens in Their Treaty Rights?"; (3) "Arbitration Treaties That Mean Something"; and (4) "Experiments in Federation for Judicial Settlement of International Disputes." In these lectures, he expressed his hope that a world court would be established to which all nations would be willing to submit controverted "justiceable questions." Such questions were described by him as those capable of solution by application of the principles of international law or equity.

Taft became an active member of the World Court League, and attended several of its congresses; and he was the President of the League to Enforce Peace from its organization on June 17, 1915, until 1921. In nearly all parts of the country he spoke in behalf of a World Court and of a League. He spoke at the Lake Mohonk peace conference on May 17, 1916, where he described himself "as a missionary for the League to Enforce Peace." Branches of this League were formed in many sections of the United States, and Taft traveled extensively to attend meetings of these regional branches and to speak at them. After diplomatic relations with Germany were broken off (February 3, 1917), he divided his time between advocating the winning of

4. New York, Charles Scribner's Sons, May, 1914.

the war, and what in the second World War has come
to be called the winning of the peace. This went on
steadily until the opening of the Paris Peace Conference (January 11, 1919), and the emergence of
specific proposals for a League of Nations. Most of his
articles in the *Philadelphia Public Ledger*, from January
30, 1918, to April 30, 1919, were on the proposed
League of Nations. He headed a group of speakers
which toured the country beginning in February, 1919,
in support of the League; and from February to April,
1920, he spoke almost daily in the Middle West and
South, trying to arouse public support for entrance of
the United States into the League.

Despite the political rancor aroused by the inclusion
of the League Covenant in the Treaty of Versailles
and the consequent question whether it should be
ratified by the United States Senate, with, or without
reservations, Taft was entirely disinterested in his
advocacy of the League. His brother Horace Dutton
Taft, in his *Memories and Opinions*[5] says of his great
effort:

"It was inevitable that a man of his temperament
should enthusiastically welcome a method of deciding
international disputes by legal methods, as it was inevitable that [T. R.] Roosevelt should scorn such
methods and seek for justice, that is, our view of it,
with the sword. My brother had no love for Wilson,
but he felt that this question, big with the fate of the
world, was too vast for personal or party considera-
tions. Since the Philippine days there had been no such
exhausting experience as the speech-making trip of the

5. New York, Macmillan Company, 1942, p. 125.

group of which he was the leader. The constitutional requirement of two-thirds in the Senate was too much of a handicap and we followed our isolationist path to its natural ending. I gloried in his single-minded devotion to the noblest of causes when bitter partisanship and rancorous personal hatred fatally warped the minds of so many."

One of the charges made, reflecting on his disinterestedness, was that Taft had been financed by the Carnegie Foundation in his tour in 1919 in support of the League of Nations. The denial of this charge, as reported in the *Journal-Courier*, February 24, 1919, was made by Robert S. Houston, treasurer of the League to Enforce Peace, who said, "Not only has Mr. Taft not received a dollar from the Carnegie Foundation, but he has never received a dollar from the League for his services. On the contrary, he has been a constant and generous contributor to our funds in addition to his incalculable contributions of time and work. The opposition senators will not help their case by cheap and false slurs against President Wilson and ex-President Taft." An amusing incident which occurred in Detroit, Michigan, on April 1, 1919, would indicate that no elaborate financial arrangements had been made for his trip. It is reported in the *Journal-Courier*, April 2, 1919, that, stopping over in Detroit on his way to speak in Kalamazoo on the League of Nations, Taft ran out of change, and walked a mile to the city hall to ask Mayor Couzens to cash a check.

A selection of Taft's speeches and articles on the League of Nations, delivered and written between May 12, 1915, and April 28, 1919, edited by Theodore Marburg and Horace E. Flack, was published in 1920 by the Macmillan Company, with the title *Taft Papers on League of Nations*.

After he went on the bench in 1921, he gave up public speaking.

# VII

## Taft, the New Haven Citizen

During Taft's professorship, the Taft family lived in four different New Haven houses, only two of which are still standing. One of these, on Prospect Street, he leased and lived in for five years, and the other, on Whitney Avenue, he owned and occupied for about a year and a half.

I have already referred[1] to his inquiry in December, 1912, about the "house which is next to the Farnams,. on the hill." This was Hillcrest, 367 Prospect Street, the impressive home standing in spacious grounds, which was built in 1875 by Joseph T. Whittlesey, and which is now occupied in 1945 by his daughter and her husband, Admiral Frank D. Berrien. Taft's lease of the house, beginning in September, 1913, ran for two years, and was subsequently renewed.

In the period from April 1, 1913, when they arrived in New Haven, until they left for Murray Bay, in July, the Tafts lived at the Hotel Taft. On their return to the city on September 17, 1913, they went again to the hotel, to remain there until the Whittlesey house was ready. One of the improvements made in anticipation of their occupancy was the installation of electricity. They took the house unfurnished, and Taft used the northwest front room on the first floor as his home office. The Tafts lived in this house until the middle of May, 1918, when they took up residence at 2029 Connecticut Avenue, Washington, D. C. This change was made in consequence of a leave of absence

1. Chapter I.

from the University granted so that Taft might serve as co-chairman of the National War Labor Board. The lease on the Berrien house was terminated on September 15, 1918, at Taft's request.

On their return to New Haven in the fall of 1919, the Tafts moved into the house at 70 Grove Street, which he sublet from Mrs. John Addison Porter. This house stood on the south side of Grove Street near the southeast corner of Church Street, on the plot now occupied by the rear extension of the Century Building, 265 Church Street. The property belonged to the Spaulding estate which was in process of settlement. Therefore the lease contained a sale clause, and when the house was sold in less than a year, Taft was notified that he must vacate the premises. In these circumstances, he took a step which would indicate that he intended to remain at Yale and make New Haven his permanent residence.

In December, 1919, he bought the home of Charles P. Wurts, at 113 Whitney Avenue. This stately, substantial house still stands near Bradley Street between the property of the late George H. Watrous and that of Wallace B. Fenn. It is directly opposite the New Haven County Historical Society, and in recent years has been occupied by the McKeown Whitney Secretarial School. The lot has a frontage of 65 feet, and a depth of 278 feet. The transaction was not announced in the *Journal-Courier* until April 12, 1920, when it was said that Taft had purchased the house for "residential purposes," at a price "close to $24,000." This was to be the family home, but as it turned out, Taft was to spend little time there.

On May 7, 1920, Taft was asked to become one of

the arbitrators to appraise the Grand Trunk Railway system as a preliminary to its transfer to the Canadian Government. He accepted and later, June 19, 1920, asked the University to grant him leave of absence for the academic year 1920–21. This was approved by the Prudential Committee on June 21, 1920. During most of this year, Taft was away, either on speaking tours, or in connection with his duties as arbitrator, but his headquarters were in New Haven. Occasionally he gave an address here, as on October 30, 1920, when he spoke at a political rally in Woolsey Hall. Most of the month of January the Tafts spent in Bermuda, whence they returned to New Haven on January 27, 1921.

For some reason not known to me, the Tafts vacated the Whitney Avenue house. There is a statement in the *Journal-Courier* of May 14, 1921, that "Professor and Mrs. Taft temporarily are living at 60 York Square," to which they had recently moved. This residence was known as the Southworth house. It was demolished in 1930, to make way for the Payne Whitney Gymnasium. A picture of it and its adjoining houses appears on the cover of the *Yale Alumni Weekly* for September 19, 1930.

The Tafts went to Murray Bay in June, 1921, and while there Taft was appointed Chief Justice of the United States Supreme Court. On July 29, 1921, the Taft home at 113 Whitney Avenue was sold to Mrs. Mary K. Russell, widow of Dr. Thomas H. Russell, of 79 Trumbull Street. The sale price, as announced in the *Journal-Courier* of August 2, 1921, was $25,000.

The migrations of the Taft family in New Haven from house to house are said to have given rise to a movement to raise a fund by public subscription with which to buy a home for Mr. Taft. The story goes that when Taft learned of the project, he insisted on having the collected money returned to the subscribers.

That Taft thought of himself as a citizen of New Haven, and not merely a temporary resident, was often shown by word and deed. For example, being in Cincinnati in connection with a tax matter, he is reported to have said, according to a dispatch to the *Journal-Courier* of August 15, 1913, "I am a New Haven citizen. I have already paid my taxes there and I intend to stay there, too. New Haven is good enough for me." He had occasion, however, to object to the amount of his personal tax there. On January 16, 1914, he protested the valuation placed on his automobile, $4,500. He explained that he had bought it second-hand for $2,000. To make matters worse, he had forgotten to swear in his taxes, so that a ten per cent penalty was attached.

He was sworn in as a voter in New Haven at 5.04 P.M. on October 24, 1914. There was a crowd in the City Hall to observe him. Called upon to read a part of the Constitution of the United States, he complied, whereat someone called out "Louder." For once, he failed to see the humor of the situation, and replied, "Gentlemen, I haven't come here to be made fun of. I really can read."

There were a few other times when those who were politically opposed to him did not treat him with courtesy. One such instance was on November 6, 1916. Taft had been induced to speak at a noonday political rally of employees of the Winchester Repeating Arms Company in front of the factory. When he began to speak, a part of the crowd refused to listen and tried to prevent others from hearing. "We've been listening to him since 1907, and we've heard enough of him," one loud voice complained. In answer to a remonstrance, another one said, "That's all right, but what about a former President of the United States speaking at a street corner? Do you approve of that?"[2]

Bull Moosers, of course, did not agree with him, and some others thought him too conservative. Not all were overawed by his exalted past. In an address at the Lincoln Day banquet on February 12, 1914, in the clubhouse on Crown Street of the New Haven Young Men's Republican Club, he spoke vigorously against the recall, reiterating views recently expressed in a *Saturday Evening Post* article. He told his party to stick to its principles, and not to merge with Progressives in order to get votes. This stirred W. H. Avis, a Progressive party committeeman from Whitneyville, to write a reply, which appeared in the *Journal-Courier* for February 16, 1914. Avis strongly defended Theodore Roosevelt, and said that Taft didn't get the people's viewpoint because he was a born aristocrat.

He participated in committee meetings of the local Republican organization and spoke at many of its banquets and rallies, but he declined to run for any office. On the evening of November 3, 1914, he spoke from the porch of Colonel I. M. Ullman's house on Whitney Avenue, and defended him for having pulled down pictures of President Wilson and Governor Simeon E. Baldwin at one of the polling booths in the ninth ward. The pictures had been posted illegally, he said, for electioneering purposes. On his return to New

2. *Journal-Courier*, November 7, 1916.

Haven in the fall of 1919, he spoke on the evening of September 29, 1919, at a Republican dinner in support of the candidacy for Mayor of Major James A. Haggerty. "When I was invited to come here," he said, "I hesitated to accept the invitation lest I might not have a right to figure among the workers in the party in New Haven, but coming back as I have after a year's absence, I seized upon the opportunity to give public notice that I was still a citizen of New Haven and still a Republican."

He was appointed Chief Justice of the United States Supreme Court in 1921, as a citizen of Connecticut, and not of Ohio. Until three years before her death, Mrs. Taft returned regularly to New Haven to vote.

He took great interest in foreign-born citizens. Twice, on May 12, 1914, and on May 3, 1915, he spoke in the Green Street School to large audiences of Italians, men, women, and schoolchildren. His subject was "American Opportunity." "When I was President of the United States," he said, "a bill was submitted to me to sign which excluded from this country those who could not read or write. I vetoed the bill." He advised the members of his audience to be Americans, not Italian-Americans. After the meeting, he shook hands with several hundred people. His democratic habits astounded foreign-born residents. There is a story about a Pole who stopped an American acquaintance on the New Haven Green, and pointed to the figure of Mr. Taft crossing the Green. "Where in Europe could you see anything like that?" he asked. Over the ex-President's arm was a suit of clothes which he was carrying to the tailor to be pressed.

An allied interest was one which he had for the welfare of boys. Two hundred boys were present when on the evening of February 14, 1916, he spoke at the invitation of Superintendent Richard Lovell, at the housewarming of the United Workers Boys Club on Jefferson Street. Another speaker on this occasion was Edwin P. Root. Taft was the principal speaker at a banquet on the night of October 7, 1917, to raise $24,000 for the support of this club.

He was also a strong supporter of the local Young Men's Christian Association, spoke in its support at meetings in 1915, 1918, and 1921, and helped Mr. Judson J. McKim, then General Secretary, in many other ways, including the gift of money. This he did, despite the fact that under existing regulations he could not then have become an active member of the Association, because he was a Unitarian.

One of his early public appearances in New Haven was on April 25, 1913, when, at the suggestion of George Dudley Seymour, two white oak trees were planted on the Green, back of Center Church, in commemoration of the 275th anniversary of the founding of New Haven. One of the saplings, named in honor of the Reverend John Davenport, was planted by Mr. Taft, assisted by Samuel H. Fisher; and the other, in honor of Governor Theophilus Eaton, was planted by the Superintendent of Parks, Mr. Amryhn. There is reproduced in Mr. Seymour's *New Haven* (p. 754) a picture of the principals on this occasion, including, besides Taft and Seymour, the Reverend Oscar E. Maurer, and William W. Farnam, President of the Park Board.

Immediately after his arrival in New Haven, April 1, 1913, Taft's help was sought in connection with plans for a new post office. When in Washington, on September 25, 1913, he conferred with Secretary of the Treasury McAdoo concerning these plans. On June 4, 1914, at 4 P.M. in a pouring rain, but shielded by a tent, he laid the cornerstone of the new building. A copy of his address was placed in a copper box in the stone. Taft made a strong plea that the New Haven Green be preserved intact.

He was an ardent supporter of the work of the New Haven City Plan Commission, in which George Dudley Seymour was active. He was invited to attend a meeting of the Commission to be held on June 22, 1914, and, being unable to attend, sent instead a letter which is printed in Seymour's *New Haven* (pp. 577–578). The letter urged that the city acquire control of property surrounding the Green, particularly parcels adjacent to the City Hall. This project was the subject of a hearing in the aldermanic chamber on the evening of March 8, 1915. Mr. and Mrs. Taft attended and Taft urged that in accordance with the report of the Plan Commission the Metzger and Ives property on Church Street be bought to be used for City Hall purposes. Chairman Campner presided. There was not time to hear opponents of the plan, and so no vote was taken. Chief opponents were the late Judge Albert McC. Mathewson, and Anthony Carroll. They were heard at a meeting held on March 22, 1915. The following quotation from the *Journal-Courier* of March 23, 1915, shows that considerable emotion was displayed, and that voters were not overawed by their distinguished fellow citizen:

"What attendants at the meeting will best remember are not the arguments advanced . . . but the remarks which Professor William H. Taft directed to Anthony Carroll. It might have been said to be a prolongation of the little tiff which took place between the former President and Mr. Carroll after the hearing two weeks ago in the corridors of the City Hall when Mr. Carroll attempted to cross swords with Prof. Taft, who would have none of it. [In his argument last night, Taft] had reached a point where he said the trouble with those who opposed the proposition was that they were as those looking out of an engine traveling backward, they couldn't see before them. Thereupon, Mr. Carroll interjected, 'We can see as well as you can,' and he added, 'You didn't get more than 21 electoral votes.' Hisses were uttered at this remark, and the ex-President with a broad smile on his face, answered, 'Excuse me, I didn't think I came here as a presidential candidate'; and he laughed audibly. 'I came here as a private citizen, and I have as much right here as you have, Mr. Carroll.' Applause so strenuous greeted this retort that he could hardly be heard above the din as he continued: 'The trouble with Mr. Carroll, since he has become a little personal, is that he has become so used to objecting, that he doesn't know when to favor. Every community, every project, needs a brake going down hill. But this community is no longer going down hill; it's on the road to progress. It is going up hill, and it doesn't need a brake. In fact a brake is disagreeable and an obstruction, and not only disagreeable, but makes a disagreeable noise.' Mr. Carroll did not answer, and the ex-President sat down."

Mr. Seymour says that Taft greatly loved New Haven and favored the adoption of systematic city planning and the installation of terminal facilities in the harbor. Even after he had gone to Washington and had been sworn in as Chief Justice, Mr. Taft at the request of Mr. Seymour appeared before the Committee on Military Affairs of the House of Representatives, and advocated the passage of a bill, which had been introduced by Congressman John Q. Tilson, to authorize the Secretary of War to transfer Fort Hale reservation to the City of New Haven.

His participation in New Haven campaigns to sell Liberty Bonds, and to raise money for the Red Cross, was not alone an expression of patriotism. It was also the acceptance by him of what he considered to be a duty to the community in which he lived. He was a leading speaker in such campaigns, but he was also a worker with his fellow members in the ranks and as an executive committeeman. His associates soon felt perfectly at ease with him, with no restraining consciousness that they were dealing with an ex-President of the United States. "He had a rare faculty," wrote Judson J. McKim,[3] "for recognizing and encouraging those who were carrying the burden of [such campaigns.] Many persons to this day remember with gratitude spoken or written words of encouragement which came from him so naturally when he was in the presence of those who were sincerely working on difficult civic, patriotic, and religious tasks." One of those who so remembers him and counted him as a friend is Joseph C. Johnson, who was chairman of the local committee in the Red Cross drive of March, 1916. Taft was chairman of the National Central Committee. The following letter illustrates his thoughtfulness in showing appreciation to those who worked with him.

3. McKim to Hicks, May 13, 1940.

# William Howard Taft

"New Haven, Connecticut, April 10, 1916

*"My dear Mr. Johnson:*

"Now that the Red Cross campaign is over, and you have led your forces to such a glorious victory, I write to congratulate you on the work you have done, and to take this opportunity to felicitate myself on the soundness of my view when I expressed the conviction that under your leadership, and with your noted energy and vim, the movement was bound to succeed. You have put New Haven before every other city in the country in the matter of the number of Red Cross members as compared with the population. When I saw the signs upon the billboards in my visits to and from New Haven, and read their stirring appeal, I knew someone was at work who understood, and who had the courage to meet the expense necessary to do the thing in hand. In behalf of the National Red Cross, therefore, and also personally, I write this letter to express the very great obligation that the Red Cross and the public are under to you for the effort and sacrifice you had to make to bring about this much desired end. I have also written to the ladies who helped you, Mrs. Ullman and Mrs. Buckland, to felicitate them on the result and their part in it.

Sincerely yours,<br>WM. H. TAFT"

He was at home in small groups of intellectuals as well as in large gatherings. In 1913, he was elected a member of The Club, a select group of lawyers, doctors, religious leaders, and professors, which met twice a month, in rotation, in the homes of the members. On January 7, 1914, the meeting was held in the home of Dr. George Blumer, Taft's physician. Nineteen members were present to hear Taft speak on "The Monroe Doctrine; and Mexico."

People were pleased to see him in church. Often when in the city, because there was no Unitarian church in New Haven, he attended the Yale University Sunday morning service, "sitting in a front pew at the right of the pulpit, following closely the morning sermon, participating in the singing of the songs and bowing devoutly during the prayer. I never saw a speaker conclude his service," wrote Mr. McKim, "without seeing Mr. Taft move out promptly from his pew and go over to greet the speaker to express his appreciation, in his characteristically happy manner, for the leadership of the morning service."

There was little time in his busy life for entertaining friends in his home, or for accepting purely social invitations to dine. But on such occasions, especially intimate dinners when conversation was general, he was the center of interest, and often talked freely about his experiences with notable persons. At one such dinner, given by Edward A. Harriman in honor of General Herbert M. Lord, he gave an amusing account of President Theodore Roosevelt's literary activities. As recalled by Mr. Harriman,[4] Taft said, "T. R. always had people reading for him, and when his attention was called to a book which he liked (suppose there were such a book as *Ride 'Em Cowboy*, by Abdul Amir of Denver), he would telegraph the author inviting him to luncheon at the White House. He would also ask Root and me to meet Mr. Amir, although we

4. Harriman to Hicks, May 19, 1940.

never had time to read anything, and when Root hemmed and hawed, T. R. would say: 'I know what you mean, Elihu; you mean that you will come if you have no subsequent engagement.' Then when the author came to lunch, Root and I would sit there in silence, while T. R. would say, 'Mr. Amir, I regard your account of that rodeo in Chapter Ten as one of the finest pieces of descriptive writing in literature.' The political effect of such literary appreciation on Mr. Amir is easy to imagine."

Despite his heavy schedule of engagements, he so naturally observed the amenities of social life in his daily contacts that his circle of New Haven friends grew with each new activity. Those who lived near him said that he was a good neighbor. One of them recalls an especially appealing picture of him. "He was particularly fond of children," wrote Edward G. Buckland,[5] "and our daughters, then eight and twelve years old respectively, used to wait for his coming down Prospect Street hill to go to his classes. They would join him on either side and go down with him to their school."

The relations between Taft and ex-President Theodore Roosevelt were watched by everyone with keen interest. One event of which New Haveners and indeed the whole country took special note, was the first meeting of the two men after Taft's defeat for reëlection. This took place in New Haven on April 13, 1915, at the funeral of Professor Thomas R. Lounsbury, at which both Taft and Roosevelt were honorary pall-

5. Buckland to Hicks, April 18, 1940.

THE LOUNSBURY FUNERAL, APRIL 13, 1915

bearers.[6] The local newspapers, reporting the funeral, observed nothing unusual in the actual event. "Their meeting yesterday afternoon, which took place in the vestibule of Battell Chapel a few minutes after 2 o'clock, was of a cordial nature," said the *Journal-Courier*, April 14, 1915. "Alighting from separate conveyances, Professor Taft and Colonel Roosevelt found themselves in the main corridor of the Chapel facing Elm Street, and in the midst of a group of the other distinguished bearers who were already about to take their places for the processional. Professor Taft was the first to arrive and he stood chatting in subdued tones with several of the Faculty. Colonel Roosevelt walked up the steps with Professor Brander Matthews a moment later. The ex-Presidents recognized each other at a glance and both advanced to greet each other at the same moment. Professor Taft smiled and Colonel Roosevelt replied with a smile of recognition."

After the service at the grave in Grove Street Cemetery, Roosevelt entered one carriage, and Taft another. The latter drove straight to the station, leaving immediately for Boston, where he was to dedicate a Young Men's Christian Association building.

Years afterward, William Lyon Phelps[7] recalled the event somewhat differently. Said he, "I was standing

6. The following is the complete list of honorary pallbearers: For the University administration, President Hadley and Director of the Sheffield Scientific School Russell H. Chittenden; for the American Academy of Arts and Letters, Brander Matthews and Theodore Roosevelt; for the Faculty of the Sheffield Scientific School, Professors Wilbur L. Cross and Louis V. Pirsson; for the other faculties of the University, Professors Taft and Henry A. Beers; and from the community, George Dudley Seymour and the Honorable Simeon E. Baldwin.

7. *Autobiography with Letters*, p. 618.

by the coffin in the vestibule just before the obsequies, when the two men came up from opposite sides. Roosevelt gave no sign of recognition, whereupon Taft went up to him, said, 'How are you, Theodore?' and extended his hand. Roosevelt shook hands silently without smiling; no further communication passed between them."

Another account of the meeting is given in Governor Wilbur L. Cross's *Connecticut Yankee*.[8] "When Roosevelt arrived with Brander Matthews," wrote Cross, "I was standing with other pallbearers in the outer vestibule of Battell Chapel, talking with Taft, who as soon as Roosevelt approached extended his hand to him with a 'Hello, Teddy.' Roosevelt straightened up, throwing back head and shoulders, took Taft's hand limply, and returned the informal greeting with 'How do you do, Mr. Taft?' Then he turned away to greet the other pallbearers. A minute or two later, Taft again got Roosevelt's attention and inquired after Mrs. Roosevelt's health. He was assured that she was 'very well.' In return Roosevelt learned that Mrs. Taft was very well also, and hoped that Mr. Roosevelt would call at the house after the services. Roosevelt regretted that he must leave as soon as the funeral was over. Taft was deeply hurt, as one could see, but his face quickly regained its composure."

That the last word has not been said on this meeting is indicated by the appearance from time to time of new versions of the story. George Wharton Pepper devotes nearly a page to it in his *Philadelphia Lawyer*,[9] and in his account, the greetings took place at the

8. 1943, p. 151.
9. Philadelphia, J. B. Lippincott Co., 1944, pp. 91-92.

grave, instead of at the Chapel. After referring to the estrangement between the two men, Mr. Pepper continued:

"Three years later a surface reconciliation took place. The occasion was the funeral in New Haven of Professor Thomas Lounsbury, at which both ex-Presidents were pallbearers. Lounsbury and my father-in-law had been warm friends, and my wife, who at the time of Lounsbury's death was visiting in New Haven, attended the funeral for old-time's sake. The year was 1915. She gives the following exact account of what took place:

" 'At the open grave, only ten or twelve feet in front of me, stood Mr. Taft and Colonel Roosevelt with only one other pallbearer between them. I was interested in noticing the backs of their frock coats, as they seemed to show so plainly the difference in their characters. Mr. Taft's seemed very "roomy" and was hanging loosely—perhaps because it was not buttoned; while Colonel Roosevelt's was very tightly drawn—so much so that there were horizontal creases across the back. When the service was over and after a moment of silence, they started to move away. At this moment Mr. Taft stretched out his arm in front of the intervening pallbearer and held out his hand saying, How are you, Theodore? Colonel Roosevelt, with apparent reluctance, took the outstretched hand. It was over in a twinkling but to me it was a moment of tense interest, because I knew of their long estrangement. They walked away, but not side by side.'

"After this incident there was some show of irritation by the Roosevelt family because the Colonel (it was charged) had been brought without warning into such close contact with Taft. Fortunately, Anson Phelps Stokes, then secretary of Yale University, had had charge of the funeral arrangements and, with his usual foresight, had named all the pallbearers in his telegram of invitation to Roosevelt. The fact that Taft was on the list had evidently failed to register; but when Stokes produced a copy of his telegram it became clear that if there had been any fault it was at the Roosevelt end of the line."

Pringle (p. 860), says that the meeting was "quite colorless," and that Taft wrote next day to Karger, "It was pleasant enough, but not cordial or intimate. I am glad to have . . . the status between us fixed—that of armed neutrality."

A year later, according to the *Journal-Courier*, June 29, 1916, when Taft was in New York, and was "asked if he would be willing to speak from the same platform as Colonel Roosevelt, he said, 'I am for Hughes. I would not let my personal feelings interfere. If such speaking arrangements were made, I would act as a private in the ranks and obey orders.' " The two men met next at a reception in New York given to Charles E. Hughes, on October 3, 1916. The next day Taft said, "We shook hands just like any gentlemen would shake hands." Their final meeting was in May, 1918, when they both happened to be in the Blackstone Hotel, in Chicago. Roosevelt was at dinner when Taft entered the dining room. The *Journal-Courier* of May 27, 1918, reports that Taft made his way to Roosevelt's table, they shook hands, and smiled, while other diners rose and cheered. Taft sat down and they talked for half an hour.

Roosevelt died on January 6, 1919. Taft attended

the funeral in New York City, and went to the grave.

New Haven was one of the cities which responded to the request of the American Defense Society, cooperating with the Roosevelt Memorial Committee, that the anniversary of Roosevelt's birth be observed throughout the country. A letter written by Taft in praise of Roosevelt was read and distributed to all schoolchildren in New Haven, and on Sunday evening, October 26, 1919, memorial services were held in Woolsey Hall. Hiram Bingham presided, and Taft delivered the chief address, which was quoted extensively in the *Journal-Courier* of October 27, 1919. He spoke vigorously of the need of such men as Roosevelt in 1919 to counteract the evils resulting throughout the world from the great war just ended. "It is at this juncture," he said, "that the living influence of Theodore Roosevelt and his robust and triumphant Americanism can do much for our country and for righteousness."

In concluding his address, he used the following words, which should dispel any doubt that Taft was still appreciative of the sterling qualities which Roosevelt possessed:

"Theodore Roosevelt's Americanism did not represent an unwillingness to share the responsibilities of the world with the world. He was willing and anxious that America should pull her part in the boat. When war was on, when he thought pacifists were attempting to paralyze national action, he denounced everything that bore the name peace lest it meant letting up in the fight before we were through. As the war drew to its close, however, with his usual foresight, he saw the necessity of a union of the nations in order to meet the problems that the upheaval of the war would necessarily present, and to preserve the peace so hardly won. He was in favor of a league of nations. He had suggested such a league as far back as when he received the Nobel prize, a league in which each nation would contribute lawful force to suppress lawless violence among the nations. Of course, whether he would have been in favor of the present league of nations now under discussion, no one can say, for he did not live to see the covenant. I do not suggest his attitude here as an argument for the present league; but I discuss it merely to show what his Americanism was. In his conversations, in his writings, just before his death, he recognized the necessity for such a union, and these conversations and writings entirely refute the slightest suggestion that by Americanism he meant the narrow provincialism that would exclude us from doing our part in now meeting the awful responsibilities that the war has thrust upon those who have power to help stabilize the world.

"How much we have lost in him grows upon us as the difficulties of the situation grow. He spoke to and moved the common man. The plain people, workingmen, farmers and all, believed that he felt for them and put himself in their place. In his public service, in his activities in uplifting the poor, in his expressed sympathy for the under dog in the fight for life, he had won their confidence. In such a controversy as that we are now to face, his words for American institutions and against European bolshevism, in favor of law, order and liberty and against plunder and anarchy, would have sunk deep into the heart of the plain people. Against most advocates of law and order, the bolshevistic demagogue can effectively charge capitalistic prejudice and a lack of sympathy with the masses, but not so with Theodore Roosevelt. He could appeal to workingmen over the heads of lawless leaders whom he would denounce, as he did Moyer and Haywood, as undesirable citizens, and could rouse their patriotism and better natures. What a great defender of our treasured institutions we lost in his death."

These sentiments cannot properly be characterized as insincere expressions called for by a public occasion at which only good was expected to be said of the departed. On other occasions, when no reporters were present, and when Taft was giving an intimate talk to his friends, similar views were expressed. On one such occasion at the Graduates Club in New Haven, Taft gave an account of his experiences with well-known personages. Among them were William II of Germany, Nicholas II of Russia, Pope Leo XIII, and Theodore Roosevelt. Probably half of his address was devoted to Roosevelt. In his references to Roosevelt there was not a trace of bitterness, and only one suggestion of criticism that could be reported as adverse. "He remarked, with his characteristically good-natured chuckle," wrote my informant, "that there might be some reason not to accept every one of T. R.'s statements of fact. As a whole, the address was a eulogy of Roosevelt. He indicated in many ways with what satisfaction he had himself served under Roosevelt, saying that the latter had 'no pride of opinion,' and was always ready to change a position that he had taken on presentation of new evidence and advice. Finally he said that it was a great misfortune for the country that Roosevelt had permitted himself to be a candidate for President in 1912. Had he not done this, said Taft, nothing under God's Heaven could have prevented Roosevelt's nomination and election in 1916. 'And what a war President he would have made!' These last words Taft boomed out with fine orotund effect."

# VIII

# The Chuckle and the Chairs

Talk for ten minutes with anyone who knew Taft in New Haven, and he will mention two things, Taft's chuckle, and the oversized chairs which were provided at Yale for his special use.

The best description of the chuckle is that found in Pringle's biography (p. 367), where he writes:

"A political asset of unquestioned worth lay in the subterranean chuckle which preceded Taft's frequent laughter. It was, by all odds, the most infectious chuckle in the history of politics. It started with a silent trembling of Taft's ample stomach. The next sign was a pause in the reading of his speech and the spread of a slow grin across his face. Then came a kind of gulp, which seemed to escape without his being aware that the climax was near. Laughter followed hard on the chuckle itself, and the audience, invariably, joined in. They laughed even when the point which had amused Taft was vague to them."

The chuckle was as effective in the classroom, at alumni banquets, and in serious academic addresses, as it was in political speeches. I get the impression, however, that it was not on such occasions always carried through to audible laughter. The gleam in his clear blue eyes, and the smiling expanse of his countenance were themselves enough to put his audience in good humor.

His size made him a noticeable figure anywhere. But neither his good humor nor his bulk would have been sufficient to account for his success. In fact, both of these characteristics were used by opponents in attempts to discredit him. Remembering that everybody laughs at a fat man, cartoonists used them to give the impression that he was just another good-natured fat man. Had he not been intellectually strong, with pronounced views, and the ability to express them, his size and constant good humor might have been too great a handicap. Ridicule has been the downfall of many a useful but mediocre man. Taft was not mediocre. Moreover he turned his good humor and his size to good advantage. He joked about himself, and thus took the sting out of ridicule by others. When people tell stories about Taft's size, even now, they laugh with him and not at him.

He poked fun at himself in many of his letters. Writing to Secretary Stokes on October 20, 1920, to explain that he could not accept an invitation to speak in New Haven because he had agreed to speak that night in Philadelphia, he said, "You remember the Irish member of Parliament who said that it was impossible for a man to be in two places at once, unless he was a bird, and you will bear me out in saying that I haven't many bird-like qualities." Charles G. Morris, of New Haven, remembers that at a meeting of the Executive Committee of the Connecticut Civil Service Reform Association, Horace Taft said with glee that he had just received a letter from his brother William, who wrote from Europe, "I am going to quit Banting, and let nature have her perfect work."[1]

Taft's brother, Horace, in *Memories and Opinions*

1. William Banting was a London cabinetmaker whose method of reducing corpulance by avoiding fat, starch, and sugar in food was published and much discussed in the year 1864.

# The Chuckle and the Chairs

(p. 108) tells of an incident when the three brothers, Horace, Henry, and William, went to the theater. "Will was then at his stoutest. He sat down in the very small theater seat and seemed to overflow. He looked at me smilingly and said: 'Horace, if this theater burns, it has got to burn around me.'"

Malcolm Ross in *Death of a Yale Man* (p. 369) tells how Taft used his bulk to stop a train. "Taft," writes Ross, "stuck at a water-tank railroad station and learning that the train would only stop if a number of passengers wished to come aboard, telegraphed to the conductor: 'Stop at Hicksville. Large party waiting to catch train.'" Everybody knows the story reprinted by Pringle (p. 236). After journeying up the mountains in the Philippines, to Baguio, Taft cabled Secretary of War Root:

"Stood trip well. Rode horseback twenty-five miles to five thousand feet elevation."

Root cabled back:

"Referring to your telegram . . . how is the horse?"

When Taft came to New Haven to live, he owned a Pierce-Arrow automobile. This he disposed of, saying: "I can't afford to feed that monster: it eats up too much gasoline." In place of this large car, he bought a Ford Sedan, specially built, with a wide door.

He received many honorary degrees, and his robes had to be cut to measure. No standard size would do. It has been said that "they probably contain more yardage of pure silk than any robes extant."

Leaving New Haven in 1921 to become Chief Justice, Taft left behind him physical evidence that he required a large chair, and there are several stories relating to this fact. The first antedates his acceptance of the Yale professorship. Anson Phelps Stokes called upon him at the White House late in 1912. "When I suggested to him," wrote Mr. Stokes,[2] "that he occupy a Chair of Law at the University, he said that he was afraid that a Chair would not be adequate, but that if we would provide a Sofa of Law, it might be all right."

On his first day as Professor, after he had received the "royal welcome" already described, Dean Jones of the College went to the Hotel Taft to escort Mr. Taft to his first Faculty meeting. Entering the Faculty room, as William Lyon Phelps tells the story:[3] "It appeared there was no chair in the room sufficiently large for his frame. Someone remembered that the Campus policeman, Jim Donnelley, who weighed nearly three hundred pounds, owned a colossal arm-chair. It was sent for, brought up on the elevator, and it appeared *adorned with the horns of a bull moose!* . . . Everyone, including Mr. Taft, laughed aloud."

Preparing for student functions to which Taft was invited in 1913, committees of arrangement took pains to provide large chairs for him. Charles E. Clark, now Judge of the United States Circuit Court of Appeals, 2d Circuit, remembers that he procured such a chair to be used by Taft at a Corbey Court dinner held in the Heublein Café. "Justice Beach was to bring him to the party," wrote Judge Clark,[4] "and when Beach came in a little earlier, and saw the large chair, he hastened to withdraw it and substitute an ordinary

2. Stokes to Hicks, May 10, 1940.
3. *Autobiography with Letters*, p. 609.
4. Clark to Hicks, June 14, 1940.

chair." Beach need not have been fearful that Taft would have been embarrassed.

An oversized chair was provided for Taft at the *Yale News* banquet held on April 4, 1913. The toast-master, Albert B. Crawford, now Director of the Yale Bureau of Appointments, remembers this, but was more impressed by what happened at the table. "In those days," said Mr. Crawford, "champagne was served at these dinners. Taft sat at my right. When the wine was being served, Taft turned down his glass. Then, looking at me, he turned it back again, saying, 'Perhaps, young man, you can use this.'"

Dean Jones and Dean Rogers saw to it that special chairs were made for Taft's use in committee rooms and classrooms. One of these chairs is now in the Yale University Faculty Club. It bears the following plate:

THIS CHAIR WAS BUILT FOR
WILLIAM HOWARD TAFT
KENT PROFESSOR OF LAW IN YALE COLLEGE
1913–1921
PRESIDENT OF THE UNITED STATES
1909–1913
CHIEF JUSTICE OF THE UNITED STATES
1921
USED IN A1, OSBORN HALL

This chair has a seat twenty-five inches wide, within the arms, and twenty-one inches from front to back.

A special seat was installed for him in the front row of the balcony of Woolsey Hall, the largest University auditorium. It is still there (Number 7). Concerning this seat Morris Hadley tells the following story.[5] "I

5. Hadley to Hicks, June 19, 1940.

remember one function in Woolsey Hall, at which Mr. Taft had forgotten his ticket. Incredible as it may seem, none of the ushers recognized him, and he had a hard time getting in. He had a specially wide seat in the front row of the balcony, right across the aisle from the seats my family occupied. Mr. Taft came down the aisle, accompanied by a protesting usher, who departed, apparently satisfied, after a brief whispered colloquy. Mr. Taft, as he settled in his seat, leaned across the aisle and whispered to my mother: 'I lost my ticket, but was fortunately able to establish my identity by the breadth of my beam and the corresponding breadth of this seat.' "

Taft had to avoid such fragile things as folding chairs, some "period" chairs, and armed chairs. He had to look before he sat. Theater chairs have already been mentioned. Dentists' chairs and barbers' chairs also were a problem. This is attested by George Miller, barber at the Graduates Club in New Haven. And bath tubs had to be selected with an eye for dimensions. In Pringle's biography (p. 212), is a picture of the tub used by Taft in the Philippines. Moved out of the Governor's mansion after Taft's departure, it is being used as a swimming pool by eight or ten native children. Admiral Berrien told me that one of the attractions of the house which Taft rented at 367 Prospect Street in New Haven was the presence in it of one oversized bathtub.

The much-discussed question of Taft's health and weight took a serious turn when some people said that he was lazy, and mentally logy, and seldom did things on time.

Writing concerning Taft's presidential term, Oswald

# The Chuckle and the Chairs

Garrison Villard, in his *Fighting Years*,[6] said that Taft "was a charming gentleman, one of the finest who ever entered the White House. He was kindly, well-meaning, absolutely honest, and entirely guiltless of any purpose to turn the United States over to the reactionaries. He was merely true to his training and ultraconservatism. His great vice was that he was extremely lazy and a great procrastinator—William J. Bryan called him 'The Great Postponer' and these traits led him into one pitfall after another."

Taft's brother Horace, in his *Memories and Opinions*, devoted several pages to the question whether Taft was really lazy, and whether his weight was a serious detriment to him.

After telling of some of the periods of great physical and mental strain which Taft survived, Horace wrote: "All that I can say is that a man who saw him intimately and still thought that he was lazy must have a dreadfully high standard of energy and diligence." My own listings of his activities during the years that he lived in New Haven lead to the same conclusion. It was a steady grind which was carried on despite wind and weather, despite fatigue and the simple ailments which he might have given in to. He could not have accomplished what he did if he had been lazy and if his health had been poor. The fact is that he was healthy. During the whole period I find newspaper record of only one illness. In August, 1917, he was on a speaking tour in the Middle West, and while in Clay Center, Kansas, became ill with an intestinal ailment. He was laid up for three days, abandoned his trip, and went to Murray Bay to recuperate.

6. New York, Harcourt, Brace and Co., 1939, pp. 188–189.

# William Howard Taft

He neither smoked, nor drank intoxicants. Yet he was opposed to prohibition,[7] and he served wine to his guests. As part of a dieting scheme prescribed for him just after his election as President, the amount of water which he was allowed to drink was much reduced. Out of this circumstance grew a story which Taft told to a reporter.[8] Senator Jonathan "Bourne and I," said Mr. Taft, "were dining together at Hot Springs, Virginia, just after my election and prior to my inauguration, when the newspaper correspondent, now quite well known, but then a youngster in Washington, came by and in the course of the short talk that followed, Bourne and I mentioned the fact that we had stopped drinking. The correspondent took what was said to mean that we had sworn off and the next day his paper printed a long story that was captioned in big black type 'Taft stops drinking.'

"Then the trouble started. From all parts of the country temperance organizations began to send congratulations and a conference of the Methodist ministry went so far as to designate a committee of seven Bishops to visit me and tell me how glad the Church was that I had quit drinking. I knew one of those Bishops quite well, and so I sat down and wrote him a letter. I told him that, while I was not a drinking man, and did not intend to indulge, I nevertheless intended to serve wine at dinners given to diplomats and others who drink wines with their meals as aids to digestion. I said that if with this understanding the committee still decided to visit me, I would be delighted to re-

7. See Appendix.
8. *New York Times*, December 12, 1913.

ceive them. They decided that I was too busy and never came."

Taft was temperate in his habits except in the matter of eating. It was a constant struggle to control his weight by dieting. He was 5 feet, 11 inches in height, had a large frame, and was a big man to begin with. Any relaxing of a regimen set for him had immediate results. When he was graduated from college in 1878, he weighed 225 pounds. In 1892 when he became a United States Circuit Court Judge, he weighed 270 pounds. In the Philippine Islands, he gained fifty pounds. On March 4, 1913, when he retired from the presidency, he weighed 340 pounds. Dr. Coleman of Augusta, Georgia, prescribed a diet for him, and when Taft moved to New Haven, referred him to Dr. George Blumer, then Dean of the Yale School of Medicine. In an interview reported in the *New York Times*, December 12, 1913, Taft said that Dr. Blumer had accomplished wonders.

"The diet I have followed was prescribed by Dr. Blumer. I have dropped potatoes entirely from my bill of fare, and also bread in all forms. Pork is also tabooed, as well as other meats in which there is a large percentage of fat. All the vegetables except potatoes are permitted, and of meats, that of all fowls is permitted. In the fish line I abstain from salmon and bluefish which are the fat members of the fish family. I am also careful not to drink more than two glasses of water at each meal. I abstain from wines and liquors of all kinds, as well as tobacco in every form. The last is, however, nothing unusual, for I never drink intoxicants anyway, and I have never used tobacco in my life."

# William Howard Taft

The record available shows the success of Dr. Blumer's treatment, and that Taft held his gains during the whole period:

|  | Weight in lbs. |
| --- | --- |
| 1913, March 4, | 340 |
| 1913, April 1, | 335 |
| June, | 299 |
| September, | 282 |
| November 1, | 278 |
| December 12, | 270.8 |
| 1922, November 11 | 259½ |

Dr. Blumer says that Taft absolutely followed directions to the letter. To do so, he formed the habit of accepting invitations to speak at dinners, with the proviso that he would eat before he came. During vacations at Murray Bay, Taft was under the care of Dr. James Thacher, at one time a professor in the Yale School of Medicine. When Taft moved to Washington, D. C., Dr. Blumer referred him to Dr. Thomas Claytor, of that city.

Soon after Taft came to Yale, Isadore (Izzy) Winters, former world's lightweight wrestling champion, who was then wrestling coach at Yale, and was also, as now, proprietor of a health institute in West Haven, sought to reach him by telephone. Failing to do so, Winters asked his partner, Henry Ruden, to try his luck. The latter succeeded, but did not disclose that he was speaking for Winters. The following conversation ensued:

"Hello, is this Mr. Taft?"

"Yes, this is Mr. Taft."

"Well, this is Professor Winters."

# The Chuckle and the Chairs

Not recognizing the name, Taft stalled for time, and said:—

"I'm sorry, but being new here, I don't yet know all of my colleagues. What is your department?"

"Well, Mr. Taft," Ruden replied, "I'm professor of wrestling, and I'd like to have an appointment with you to tell you about my Health Farm."

The appointment was made for three o'clock that same afternoon in the ex-President's office in the Hotel Taft. Winters kept the appointment in person. Izzy is five feet, two inches in height, and weighs 135 pounds.

"Good afternoon, Dr. Taft," said Izzy.

"Good afternoon, Professor," said Taft. "When I was in college, I was a heavy weight wrestler. What do you think my chances would be now?"

"Well, I think you are too heavy for light work, but I can put you in shape," answered Winters.

Taft agreed to become "Professor" Winters' pupil.

Wide publicity was given to these conversations when Taft recounted them in his own way at the New Haven Chamber of Commerce dinner that night. Looking about him, he pointed to ex-Governor Rollin S. Woodruff, Colonel I. M. Ullman, and others who were habitués of the Winters Health Farm, and announced that he had become a fellow student under Izzy's tutelage.

For several years, Taft went as regularly as he could to the Health Farm, where Winters gave him breathing exercises, used the vibrator on him, took him for walks, passed the medicine ball with him, and gave him massage treatment.

Taft was an ardent baseball fan. He rode horseback,

and above all he played golf. Even this innocent exercise became a matter for political consideration. When Taft was running for President in 1908, Theodore Roosevelt received protests because his candidate played "the aristocratic game of golf."[9] He played in New Haven whenever he could. William Lyon Phelps[10] told the following story of him: "That Spring of 1913 I played golf very often with him; and he was the best of company, though always keen to win. One day, when he was playing in another foursome, he came into the locker-room, banged his clubs down on the floor, and gave a snort of rage. (He never swore.) I said, 'Why, you feel worse about being beaten at golf than you did on losing the presidency!' He replied, 'Well, I do, *now!*' "

And he kept up the game as long as his health would permit. His brother Horace in his *Memories and Opinions* (p. 108) said that when Taft was nearly seventy years old and weighed nearly 260 pounds, he played thirty-six holes of golf in one day, while he was on vacation.

9. Pringle, *Theodore Roosevelt*, p. 504.
10. *Autobiography with Letters*, p. 610.

# IX

## Ex-Professor Taft

In March, 1921, the newspapers were full of rumors that Chief Justice White was about to retire, and that Taft would be appointed to succeed him. In New Haven, interest grew as the rumors spread. The *Journal-Courier* discussed the matter editorially, emphasizing the personal loss which Yale and New Haven would suffer. On March 30, 1921, it said that "New Haven and Yale take high satisfaction in the life record of Mr. Taft. A great career, a giant's intellect— all tinged with a personality so attractive and wholesome that he comes and goes among us as one of ourselves. Indeed many, deceived by his unaffected greatness, will not know until he has gone that they have been privileged to see him come and go, and live in the same town." Returning to the subject on May 20, 1921, a writer said, "The angle that concerns many is the loss of Mr. and Mrs. Taft as residents, and the depriving of the Yale Law School of his services as a teacher at a time when the strength of the Faculty is greatly adding to its prestige. Mr. Taft has manifestly enjoyed New Haven as a center of his activities, increased by the fact that his son and daughter have their homes here."

On June 20, 1921, Taft attended the Yale Law School alumni luncheon, where his statement that he expected to teach Constitutional Law "as usual" next year, was received with smiling incredulity. On June 22, he marched in the academic procession, attended the University Commencement exercises, and spoke

at the alumni luncheon. The next day, Taft and his
family left for Murray Bay. A few days later, he was
in Montreal to attend a session of the Grand Trunk
Railway arbitration. On June 30, 1921, President
Harding nominated Taft to be Chief Justice of the
United States, and the Senate immediately, in Executive session, confirmed the nomination. Interviewed in
Montreal, Taft said, "It has been the ambition of my
life to be Chief Justice, but now that it is gratified, I
tremble to think whether I can worthily fill the position and be useful to the country. . . . I shall have to
resign my professorship of Federal Constitutional Law
at Yale, the presidency of the League to Enforce
Peace, and my position as occasional editor on the
staff of the *Public Ledger* of Philadelphia." Commenting on this news, an editorial in the *Journal-Courier* of
July 1, 1921, concluded with the words, "There is no
higher tribute to Mr. Taft than that in New Haven
where he is known so well there is no one who questions
for a moment his fitness, and more, the desirability of
the appointment." Taft remained in Montreal until
the conclusion of the Grand Trunk argument, left for
Washington on July 11, and was sworn in as Chief
Justice on the 12th.

Had this appointment taken effect during a session
of the University, there would undoubtedly have been
a student demonstration in his honor comparable to
the royal welcome that he received in 1913. Under the
circumstances, there could only be letters of resignation and of acceptance, and resolutions of congratulation and respect. From the Ritz-Carlton Hotel in
Montreal, July 1, 1921, he wrote by hand to President
Angell as follows:

# Ex-Professor Taft

*"My dear President Angell:*

"In view of my appointment as Chief Justice and my qualification for the office in a few days, I beg herewith to tender to you and the Corporation of Yale my resignation as Kent Professor of Law in Yale College. I am sorry that I should be going just as you are coming; but at any rate, there will have been an interval in which we were colleagues if only one of a few days. I cherish a fond recollection of my eight years as a member of the Yale faculty and am grateful for the consideration always shown me by the Corporation and my fellow members of the faculty.

With confident hope of the great success which awaits your administration, believe me, with respect and good wishes,

Sincerely yours,<br>Wm. H. Taft."

On the same day he wrote to Dean Thomas W. Swan, of the Yale Law School:

*"Dear Dean Swan:*

"I have just sent my resignation to President Angell as Kent Professor of Law in Yale College. I am going to qualify as Chief Justice in a few days if I carry out my plan and I wish to stand forth without relation. I am going to take the veil. Had I been disappointed, I would have greatly welcomed resuming my relations with you and think I could have done better work. But it was not to be. I am proud of having been a member of your faculty. Yours is the coming law school, and I have every confidence in the useful function you are to perform in the field of progress in the law. I regret to sever our personal relations as members of the same faculty. Please express my regret and best wishes to your colleagues.

Sincerely yours,

WM. H. TAFT"

The resignation having been made known to the Prudential Committee of the University, that body on July 16, 1921, "Voted, that the resignation of Hon. William H. Taft as Professor of Constitutional Law in the Law School and Kent Professor of Law in the College, be accepted and that the Acting Secretary [Thomas Wells Farnam] be requested to convey to Mr. Taft the congratulation of the Corporation upon his appointment as Chief Justice of the United States and their appreciation of this further honor he has brought to the University through his long career of public service."

Taft's official connection with the University did not end here. In fact, his resignation made it possible for him to accept election to membership in the Corporation, an office which he had felt himself obliged to relinquish when he became a professor in 1913. He served from 1922 to 1925, but declined the nomination for another term. President Angell invited him to speak at the alumni luncheon in June, 1925, but he was unable to accept. His letter of June 11, 1925, to President Angell is as enthusiastic an expression of loyalty to Yale as any statement made in his younger years. "I must decline with real regret," he wrote. "The essence of the Yale spirit finds its sincere expression on these occasions, and good Yale men are made better Yale men, and their vows of loyalty are renewed. It is a life-giving time. But in conforming to a needed regimen after the constant labor of a hard court term, I must forego the constant joy I have ever had in Commencements. . . . It would have been a great honor and pleasure to have continued on the Corporation, had the alumni been willing to select me; but I knew that I could not, consistently with my judicial duties, attend the Corporation meetings, and therefore I withdrew my name. I did it with great regret. I would have been delighted to take part in the deliberations of Yale's governing body, as she goes on to greater and greater accomplishments. I would have been glad to hold up your hands in the very heavy task of leadership of this great institution. You have to pilot the ship of Yale so that the great momentum it has acquired shall be directed to confer on its coming sons, and on the country we love, the highest usefulness. We are all advised of the crisis presented in the sequelae of the War and the new issues thrust on our community. The problems presented are not to be solved in *laissez faire* methods; they are to be grappled with high courage, tenacious purpose and a sense of deep responsibility to society in the preservation of law and government. This makes the burden you have to carry greater than that of any of your predecessors.

"You have behind you the united Corporation and the whole body of the Alumni, and success will certainly attend you. A University President, like the Head of the Nation, is called to account by every element affected by his administration and can not expect to escape the outcries of the selfish, the sensational busybodies and the extremists, but it is marvelous how highly unimportant much of what seems formidable of the momentary agitation becomes, in the retrospect. The strength of the University is in the traditions of Yale College and the spirit of her sons, which will always be preserved, and you, building on that foundation, are making her progress as a University worthy of its base. My heart goes out to you and Yale."

In the year 1917, Mr. Taft had given to the Yale Law Library 1,250 volumes of American law reports. In 1926, he came across additional volumes that belonged with these sets, and he sent them on to the Law School. On December 27, 1926, writing concerning these books, to Professor Edwin Borchard, then serving as law librarian, he showed his appreciation of a former colleague by the following comments on the appointment of Dean Thomas W. Swan to be a judge of the United States Circuit Court of Appeals:

"I am very sorry you are going to lose Dean Swan. He was being pressed for the District Judgeship, but while it had its attractions, he concluded to remain in the Deanship. But the present position is one I have no doubt that is of wider influence and better adapted to his tastes. I presume that he will stay as Dean until another one can be secured. It will be difficult to fill his place, for he combines a lot of qualities that are essential to a good Dean and that are not always united in learned professors and competent teachers. Of course my loyalties are divided. I think we are getting a great addition to our Federal Judiciary, and for that reason I am very glad he has accepted, but I realize how for the time being at least it cripples the Yale Law School."

His confidence in the work done by the school is shown by the fact that beginning in August, 1924, and extending to 1929, the following men, all graduates of the Yale Law School, were chosen by him to be his law clerks: C. Dickerman Williams, LL.B. 1924; Hayden N. Smith, LL.B. 1925; William W. Crosskey, LL.B. 1926; Leighton Homer Surbeck, LL.B. 1927, and John E. Parsons, LL.B. 1929. By this means he kept in touch with the affairs of the school, as well as by conversations with former colleagues and students whom he was glad to have call upon him in Washington. In general, he approved of its course of action, but he indignantly protested to President Angell when members of the Law Faculty publicly advocated a rehearing in the Sacco-Vanzetti case.

Taft's last appearance at Yale was at the Commencement in June, 1928. On the 18th he attended the annual Law School luncheon. Richard C. Hunt was the toastmaster, and the other speakers besides Taft were Judge Swan, Dean Robert M. Hutchins, and Fleming James, Jr. Taft spoke in high praise of the administration of Judge Swan as Dean of the Law School, and said that Dean Hutchins had youth, strength, courage, and real ability to administer the affairs of the school. This he said, despite his irritation at the stand taken by Hutchins in behalf of Sacco and Vanzetti. The text of his speech, the last but one which he ever made, is the following:[1]

"We have taken a wise step in solving our problem of membership [in the school] by cutting it down to those who are able to do the work of the school well. The legal profession will be made a learned profession by the use of the Honors scholarship system.

1. The manuscript of this speech, corrected by Taft, is in the Yale Law Library.

# William Howard Taft

"One remark I would like to make for the benefit of those who come to the Bar from these great law schools, where independence of thought, original research and critical examination of authorities are encouraged, and that remark relates to manners. When the young gentlemen get into court and seek to establish the correctness of the arguments they press they will not help their arguments by contemptuous reference to the court or courts whose decision they seek to reverse. It is entirely within their power to point out the errors of which they complain without attempting to emphasize their views by language personally derogatory to the mental capacity of the judges whose conclusions they would controvert. The free language of the recitation room and the uncomplimentary comment upon opinions in the class may mislead those just from that atmosphere into the use of this in court briefs.

"We have had several instances of this which we have had to restrain by admonition to counsel and an intimation that a repetition of such bad manners toward a judge or court may require discipline. Indeed it would be a good warning by Professors and Instructors to tell these budding members of the Bar that nothing is added to the argument but rather is it weakened by such a departure from courtesy and proper respect for the members of the courts of justice. An argument that cannot win its way to a successful conclusion without abuse or contemptuous reflection upon the judges of a court under review is not likely to be highly regarded. They should know—even if from the language of criticism used by their wiser instructors they have not as high an opinion of the judges as is desirable—that these judges are the only ones we have and we must treat them with that in mind. As Professor Gray of Harvard used to say, it is the business of the lawyers to tell their clients how judges will decide cases. That business will hardly be in safe hands if entrusted to those who yield to the temptation to treat rudely the reasoning or conclusions of judges with which they do not agree.

"There has been much procedural revision by judicial committees in England and I am glad to know of the reported plans for such procedural changes here. We have in this country enough judges and courts to do the work at hand if they could be properly assigned and distributed from time to time to meet the arrears at the congested centers. This is a question of the legislature giving the judges the power in themselves to make strategic distribution for this purpose. The members of a legislature who fail to see how the business which they create can be disposed of are really responsible for much of the present situation.

"Many states have formed judicial councils for reshaping their judicial procedure. The Chief Justice of Connecticut recently wrote me and asked for letters to English judges and barristers who could and would make suggestions on this head to a representative of the court visiting London in planning for this State such co-operation as could be given with the aid of the English councils.

"It is a pleasure to me to know that the Honors System which the Yale Law School adopted, the first among American law schools, has been followed by the invitation from the Connecticut Judicial Council to the honor students of the Yale Law School to aid in the judicial reforms planned in this State."

Two days later, June 20, 1928, he spoke at the alumni luncheon in the Yale dining hall. President Angell presided, and other speakers were ex-president Hadley, and Paul Claudel, upon whom had been conferred the honorary degree of Doctor of Letters. Since this was Taft's last public address, it is given below, with President Angell's introductory remarks, in the form in which it was printed in the *Semi-Centenary Record of the Class of* 1878 (pp. 18–20):

"In calling on the last of our speakers," said President Angell, "I find myself somewhat perplexed as to the degree of detail into which I should go in his biography. It may not be known to you that he began life as a heavyweight wrestler. (*Laughter.*) And I cannot but think that if his career had begun in the present year he might perhaps have emulated the leading pugilist of our day and have become a professor of English at Yale. (*Laughter and applause.*) As it was, he followed other courses and has occupied almost literally every important post in the Federal Government, winding up with the great and honorable position which he adorns today, and having on the way, as a mere way-station, occupied the Presidency. By common consent he is the most eminent of Yale alumni, first in war, first in peace, and always first in the hearts of Yale men, the Chief Justice. (*The audience arose and applauded.*)"

### Taft's Response

"Mr. President and Fellow Yale Men: It is now, if I count right, about four years since I have had the pleasure of inflicting myself on you. There was a time when the alumni of Yale couldn't avoid hearing from me by any change of Class Anniversary. But now things are different, and I congratulate you. (*Laughter.*)

"It is a really great pleasure to come back again to this fountain of youth. I observe that you have changed some of the arrangements here and you have taken away the privilege of the Anniversary class that they could say that they had been out of Yale for fifty years. We used to have an Alumni Meeting on Tuesday morning, and those who had been out seventy years or fifty years—it isn't quite equal to seventy, fifty years—were permitted to come up on the platform and sit there with the worthies of the College. That is gone from us. The truth is that we are a little bit jealous of the fact that we are not made so much of as we used to be. There are a lot of the classes here, like '68 and '73, that seem to think that they are part of the show. (*Laughter.*)

"I remember fifty years ago responding for the Class, and that William Dean Howells was the guest of the University at that time. And that prompts a review, a reminiscence, of the many who have featured in these great University meetings. And among others I think perhaps I should refer to the death of a man who was Yale in his essence, and who, when he died, remembered Yale with a legacy of a million dollars, without anything to restrict the use of that sum. Chauncey Depew has gone from us. He was a Yale man in whom we took great pride. He was a 33d Degree Mason, which is the highest, I believe, of the Scottish Rite. They are building a great Masonic monument to George Washington on the banks of the Potomac, looking towards the city that he founded, and that monument is to be crowned by a great tower rising three or four hundred feet into the sky, and looking towards the Washington Monument and the Capitol. That tower is to be called the Chauncey Depew Tower. (*Applause*.) So that when you come to Washington you may know that he is still remembered in a form that will be permanent.

"Now when you reach seventy years, in spite of the real youth that you feel, there is a movement, a prompting, to take account of stock, and you are constantly reminded of the language put upon the tomb of Elihu Yale:

> Born in America, in Europe bred,
> In Afric' travelled, and in Asia wed.
> Much good he did, some ill, so hope all's even.
> And that by mercy his soul has gone to Heaven.

Now there is great satisfaction to me in the general average that is stated in that poem, because if you look into Elihu's life you will find that this is a very optimistic view of one part of his life (*laughter*), and therefore, when we have reached seventy, we are hoping in '78 that when our call comes we will strike the same kind of average. (*Laughter*.)

"We have approved, as a Class, of all that has gone on at this Commencement. I used to be, when I was honored by membership in the Corporation, on the Committee on Degrees, and in looking back over this Commencement, I am bound to admit that, in the selection of those to be honored, I couldn't have done any better myself. I think it was great, and I think we ought to congratulate ourselves that there was arranged such a feast as that to which we were led by Bill Phelps, D.D. (*Laughter.*)

"We have passed through a great crisis for Yale. Under the leadership of President Angell, of Treasurer Day, and of Otto Bannard, we have raised $21,000,000, and there were those of us who hesitated much as to whether that could be accomplished. But it has been done and all Yale men are thoroughly grateful to those whose energy and organization made it possible. (*Long applause.*) I don't wish to minimize the material improvement and the real improvement that that will bring about. Now we have a great plan: we have a great fund for the increase of professors' salaries and for the increase of the faculty and the enlargement of their usefulness, and the question that arises in our minds when we contemplate all this new opportunity of giving a sound and useful education and of stimulating learning is, how much benefit is to be derived from it? Are the people who should get the education the ones who will improve by it? Are they who come here to appreciate the chance that they have to become cultured men and citizens of the United States, or are they going to miss that opportunity? Now there has been a great demand for university education. Is that demand for *real education* or does it come from those in these wealthy days who desire to be classified as University men for social purposes, and not for the benefit of the country in the use of the education that they should have? (*Applause.*)

"I am glad to think that we have limited to a proper number those who are going to be here, and that the system of limitation is being bettered so that we shall diminish the number of those who come here for the purpose of getting through with the least work possible in order that they may be known as Yale men. I am glad to believe that education is being more and more pressed upon those who go through the form of graduation, if they can ever get through. (*Laughter*.) It doesn't help them, and it doesn't help the University to have men go through and 'get by' by the skin of their teeth, rejoicing that they can get through in any easy way. And I am sure that the system that is now being adopted will enable us to offer the finest education to those who will improve it, and that those who will not improve it will be left by the wayside where they ought to be. The truth is that there are a good many whose motive in entering the University is not one that makes them desirable students.

"I have a theory—I don't know that it will work out—that we ought to adopt in the University, or at least advise those who are to be educated in the University to adopt, and that is that there is another profession that ought to be encouraged here, and that is the profession of the professional politician. I am in favor of all learned professions, but I am in favor of making the career of the professional politician a learned profession. (*Applause*.)

"We have gone on in a way that I can't recount in increasing the wealth of this country. Enormous fortunes are made—and fortunes that are not enormous but are nevertheless large enough by natural descent and division to the next generation—and these fortunes give a great many young men who are capable of going through college and who do go through college, the opportunity to live and not to worry themselves as to how they are going to get enough to live on themselves and have their families live in fair comfort, and to educate their children. The number of men of that kind is increasing, and unless we make these men useful in professional politics we are not doing the best with the material that is offered to us.

"Now I have had this matter called much to my attention, by being consulted by a number of young men who say, 'I want to do something: I want to help the country, but I can't get into politics.' I had a young man come to me, descended from one of the greatest men in this country as I take him to be, and he said to me: 'I was at Annapolis and I left the Navy and went into business. I was very fortunate and now my wife and I and our children are free from the obligation to look after the means of living, and I want to get into politics.' 'Well,' I said, 'why don't you?' 'Well,' he said, 'what I want to do, what I would like to do, is to be made Assistant Secretary of the Navy.' (*Laughter.*) 'Well,' I said (to use an expression that I learned in college), 'What are your chances?' He wasn't able to tell me exactly and then, so to speak, I went for him. I said, 'You are seeking, as you say, to help the country in politics. You are able to live without office; you are able to go into politics and work for the only object that you ought to have in politics, and that is to better the government around you.' 'Yes,' he said, 'but where can I begin?' I said, 'You can begin by living in a decent, respectable community, and then find out how that is governed; then go to it.' 'But,' he said, 'I can't do anything of that sort.' 'Yes, you can,' I said, 'if you devote yourself to it, if you study, if you go to every caucus and every council meeting, and if you devote yourself to that business as a professional politician; even if you don't get beyond your county, you will be doing something that you can look back upon with the thought that you have been doing something for your country. It isn't important that you should be head of a Department at Washington; you probably wouldn't be as good a man as others in that place, but you can, right in your own center and at your own home see to it that there is one man that is trying to do his best for the people around him (*applause*), and that he doesn't make his success dependent upon his getting the office that he naturally seeks for.' I said to him, 'My dear sir, I want to emphasize to you that there are a great many worse things than being defeated for office.' (*Laughter and applause*.) And I know it. And we have got to use that kind of material.

"It isn't that there are enough of that kind of men to make all the politicians, the Lord knows. But we can use an element of that sort to help along. The truth is, and I am sorry to say so, that there are a good many who think that it is entirely justifiable for a man to vote contrary to his sentiments if his vote is likely to endanger his re-election, and this is accepted often as a real moral basis for change.

"Now the more of the kind of men that I have described that we can get into the training of professional politicians the better. A professional politician is not a corrupt politician; he is not a man who is in politics only for the securing of office. A professional politician should be a man who is sufficiently experienced in the ways of politics to know how he can make his work effective to carry on the business, and the better business, of government. That is what a professional politician should be, and I think we have material here in the education that we give at Yale, and with the good fortune that may come to many who have not thrust upon them the obligation of earning a living, to devote themselves to that particular cause, and if they do they will create a profession that will inure to the benefit of the country. (*Applause.*)"

Mr. and Mrs. Taft made the trip from Murray Bay to New Haven in this June of 1928, not only to see and take part in the formal Commencement exercises, but drawn there even more strongly to attend the fiftieth reunion of Taft's college class of 1878. The headquarters of the class were in Suites 117 and 119 of the Hotel Taft. The Tafts arrived on Sunday, June 17. Taft sat on the platform that day at the annual meeting of Yale-in-China, called there by the presiding officer, his former colleague, Anson Phelps Stokes. Monday afternoon, at its headquarters, the class held a reception attended by many notables of New Haven and of the University. Tuesday, after the conclusion of the College Commencement exercises, the class went by trolley to Yale Field to attend the Yale-Harvard baseball game. "We had intended," wrote the class secretary, Ernest C. Johnson,[2] "to be the observed of all observers by marching around the field in common with the younger classes, with the Chief Justice leading the procession. But, alas, 'the best-laid schemes o' mice and men gang aft a-gley.' The rain, which had been threatening all the morning, began just as we reached the field. Taft could see no reason why we should not march just the same; but the committee,

2. *Semi-Centenary Record of the Class of 1878*, p. 14.

fortunately, overruled the Supreme Court and we went directly to our seats."

Tuesday evening the class dinner was held. Thirty-seven members, out of the original class roster of 132, were present. Judge John Proctor Clarke was the toastmaster, and Taft was the first speaker. In the *Semi-Centenary Record*, beginning at page 23, the class secretary printed comments on those who were present. Of Taft, he said (p. 27):

"Taft, large of mind and big of heart, our world-famed classmate is always most happy to show his love for '78 and to share in its fellowships and festivities. While his health is 'below average' he took a 'high stand' in traveling from Murray Bay to New Haven. It is not easy to say whether he or the class experienced the greater pleasure from this renewed association. His comments among classmates on certain current historical matters were most illuminating." Of Mrs. Taft the *Record* said (p. 29): "While not as conspicuously enthusiastic as her famous husband, she nevertheless gets a quiet enjoyment out of her association with the '78 family. She tries to take good care of Bill." In the "Personal Reports from Members," printed in the *Record*, Taft said (p. 79):

"I am a member of the Unitarian Church, and always have been. My father and mother were both Unitarians ever since I knew them.

"I have only had one wife, and am grateful that she is still living and in good health.

"I greatly enjoyed the Fiftieth-Year Reunion. The boys did not seem to me to be so old, but the fact that the majority had gone before was strongly impressed.

"Yale and '78 have been a great part of my life.

"My health is frail, because I have fibrillation of the heart and have to be careful about not overdoing in either physical or mental exercise. The Lord has been very kind to me, and I hope I am duly grateful. I am an optimist."

Taft attended every reunion of his class, except three, up to and including 1928. In college, his classmates affectionately nicknamed him "Big Pork" and "Billy." Two of his mates, Henry M. Hoyt and Howard C. Hollister, are credited with being the original "Taft-for-President" men.[3] Eighty members of his class attended Taft's inauguration as President on March 4, 1909, and the first social function held by the Tafts in the White House was a tea given to his classmates and their families at 5 P.M. on the day of his inauguration. On March 4, 1911, he entertained the class at dinner in the White House.

To the last, he retained his exuberant college spirit. Samuel H. Fisher says that once when Taft was in New Haven to attend a meeting, Yale was about to play the University of Maryland for the first time. "He asked me if it would be a good game, and if Yale was very sure to win, because he found he had to consider his heart, and he could not sit through a Harvard or Princeton game. I told him I thought it was safe for him to see the game, but, unfortunately, it turned out to be one of the closest and finest games of the season. His attitude always seemed to me an interesting proof of Taft's devotion to his Alma Mater." Hampered as he was by the state of his health, he did not lose his sense of humor. On one of his last attendances at Com-

3. *Tricennial Supplement to Quarter-Centenary Record of the Class of 1878*, p. 98.

mencement, he was sitting in Woodbridge Hall, on the street floor, where other members of the Corporation were being invested with their gowns. He had not felt equal to going up stairs. To George Dudley Seymour, he said, "I have got to go easy—my heart isn't too good, and also," he added, with a chuckle, "one of my shoe-laces has become untied, and I don't know how I am going to get it tied." Paraphrasing a New Testament verse, Seymour replied, "May I be thought worthy to fasten the latchet of your shoe?" Whereupon, he sank to his knee and fastened the lace. "I think I'll have to keep you with me always for this purpose," said Taft.

Mr. Taft died on March 8, 1930, and he was buried in the Arlington National Cemetery. On April 12, 1930, the President and Fellows of Yale University adopted the following resolution:

"Greatly loving he was greatly loved. When the news came that his life-work was over, he had a nation for his mourner.

"We of the Yale fellowship share the nation's sorrow. Yet to us his passing brings a more intimate pang, for to a degree made possible only by his personal loyalty and affection, he belonged to Yale. Chosen to the Yale Corporation in 1906, reëlected for a second six-year term in 1912, he was reëlected again for a three-year term in 1922. In 1913, after his retirement from the Presidency, he became Kent Professor of Law in Yale College, resigning from the Corporation for this purpose, and accepting appointments as Professor of Constitutional Law in the Law School and as Page lecturer in the Sheffield Scientific School. After a year's absence for war duty, he returned to his Yale professorship, from which in June, 1921, he went to the United States Supreme Court, the position in which he rendered the most distinguished service of his distinguished career. What his counsel meant to his colleagues of the Corporation, is known only to the older men who had the privilege of personal association with him during his term of office. But in the truest sense all Yale men claimed him as their counsellor. His presence at Commencement after Commencement, where, whoever else was speaker, his words of wisdom and cheer left abiding memories, was but a symbol of that pervasive influence which made him the most dearly beloved, as he was the most deeply trusted, son of Yale. We shall remember him always. We shall love him always. We shall always be the better for what he was.

"To repeat to Yale men the incidents of William Howard Taft's life would be to retell a familiar story. Others have recorded, and will long continue to celebrate, the history and achievements of one who to a degree greater than that of any Yale man in the memory of men now living expressed in his own person what Yale men like to think the true Yale man should be— A fine scholar, salutatorian and class orator of his class, a robust personality, physically as well as morally and intellectually, a friend, trusted and beloved as few men have been loved and trusted, he carried from college into the public life which early claimed him the sense of responsibility to church and state which Yale has ever held up as the ideal of her sons. Holding successively more positions of responsibility than have come to any single citizen in the history of the Republic— Solicitor General, Governor of the Philippines, Secretary of War, President, and finally Chief Justice—he brought to each new post that fine sense of justice and that consistent subordination of self to duty which made him everywhere a man to be trusted. A great friend, he proved that friendship has perennial vitality and can maintain its continuity in the face of the most painful misunderstanding. Sincerely religious he left no one in doubt as to his faith in God."

Memorials of Taft at Yale University include two oil paintings, already mentioned,[4] law books which he presented to the Law School in 1917 and 1926, various letters and papers, some of which are holographic, and the Taft Law Library Endowment Fund, established by law alumni in his honor on June 12, 1941.

On the third floor of his house in Washington, Taft had his study. It contained a small library of law reports of the Federal Courts, and some English reports; a portrait of his father, Alphonso Taft, Yale A.B. 1833; and framed autographed photographs of all justices of the Supreme Court during his Chief Justiceship. After the death of Mrs. Taft, May 22, 1943, the books were given to Bryn Mawr and Swarthmore Colleges, the portrait of Taft's father went to the Cincinnati University Law School, and the signed photographs came to the Yale Law School, to which came also a portrait bust of Taft which had been placed in the room after his death. This bust was modeled from life, in London, by Bryant Baker, in June and July, 1922, when Taft was in England to receive an honorary degree from Oxford University. Another memento, now in the Memorabilia Room in the Yale University Library, is the United States flag which was draped over Mr. Taft's casket at his funeral.

4. Chapter II.

# APPENDIX
## Taft on Prohibition

*Two Letters Written by Taft, in Opposition to the Prohibition Amendment. Reprinted from the New Haven Journal-Courier, September 7, 1918*

FORMER President William H. Taft has issued a characteristically frank and vigorous letter against the proposed prohibition amendment to the United States Constitution. The letter is addressed to Allen B. Lincoln, formerly of New Haven and now residing in Hartford, and a well-known advocate of prohibition for many years.

It appears that several weeks ago Mr. Lincoln wrote to Professor Taft a personal letter, in which he stated that "in going about Connecticut and expressing interest in the proposed prohibition amendment, I felt everywhere that your opposition to the amendment was more effective against it in Connecticut than any other adverse influence which I encountered, and because of my intense personal interest in this question for the last thirty years I was anxious to know the reasons for your opposition—not for publication, but for my own personal consideration, because I had the highest respect for your judgment and absolute confidence in your integrity in any attitude you might take. You were kind enough to send the enclosed letter in reply. As soon as I received it I realized there was no reason why it should not be published if you were willing, and I felt that it was important that something of the kind should be published in order that the full value of your opposition may be met in Connecticut as soon as possible. May I add that, after all, your concession of the soundness of the principle would really turn out to be a great help to the cause. You have said yourself in relation to the problem in Russia

# William Howard Taft

that the great American people can do whatever it undertakes to do, and I believe that the same can be true as to the practicability of prohibition."

Following is the letter which Mr. Taft had at first sent:

"New Haven, Conn., June 8, 1918.

"*My dear Mr. Lincoln:*

"I am opposed to national prohibition. I am opposed to it because I think it is a mixing of the national government in a matter that should be one of local settlement. I think sumptuary laws are matters for parochial adjustment. I think it will vest in the national government and those who administer it so great a power as to be dangerous in political matters. I would be in favor of state prohibition if I thought prohibition prohibited, but I think in the long run, except in local communities where the majority of the citizens are in favor of the law, it will be violated. I am opposed to the presence of laws on the statute book that cannot be enforced and as such demoralize the enforcement of all laws. If I were in a local community in which I thought prohibition could be enforced, I would vote for it. If not I would favor a high license, but I am not in favor of a national amendment which should force twelve or fifteen great states into a sumptuary system which the public opinion and the real practices of the people of those states would not support. I think it is most unwise to fasten upon the United States a prohibitory system under the excitement of the war, which I do not hesitate to say, every sensible supporter of prohibition in the end will regret. Let the states which wish to do so prohibit. They have every means now of enforcing prohibition. There is a federal law, sustained as constitutional, which forbids the importation into them of liquor from other states and the whole field is open to state legislation and its enforcement. I don't drink myself at all, and

. 146 .

# Appendix

I don't oppose prohibition on the ground that it limits the liberties of the people. I think that in the interest of the community and of the man who cannot resist the temptation to drink in excess, if he has the opportunity to drink at all, other citizens in the community may be properly asked and compelled to give up drinking, although that drinking may do them no injury. My objections to prohibition are as I have stated them above."

### Second Letter from Mr. Taft

Later Colonel Norris G. Osborn, editor of the *New Haven Journal-Courier*, asked Mr. Taft for an expression concerning the prohibition amendment, and Mr. Taft replied that he had already sent such an expression to Mr. Lincoln. Mr. Lincoln thereupon inquired of Mr. Taft whether the letter of June 8 could be released for publication, and Mr. Taft has sent the following reply:

"Pointe-a-Pic, P. Q., Canada, Sept. 2, 1918

"*My dear Mr. Lincoln:*

"You ask me if you may hand to Mr. Osborn, for publication, my letter to you of June 8, 1918, on national prohibition. There are some reasons for my views which I would have elaborated, had I expected the letter to be published. Therefore, please publish with that letter the following:

"A national prohibition amendment to the federal Constitution will be adopted against the views and practices of a majority of the people in many of the large cities, and in one-fourth or less of the states. The business of manufacturing alcohol, liquor and beer will go out of the hands of law-abiding members of the community, and will be transferred to the quasi-criminal class. In the communities where the majority will not sympathize with a federal law's restrictions, large numbers of federal officers will be needed for its enforcement. The central government now has very wide war powers. When peace comes, these must end, if

the republic is to be preserved. If, however, a partisan political head of the internal revenue department, or of a separate
department created for the purpose, shall always be able
through federal detectives and policemen, to reach into
every hamlet, and to every ward, and to every purlieu of a
large city, and use the leverage of an intermittently lax and
strict enforcement of the law against would-be dealers in
liquor and their patrons, he will wield a sinister power,
prospect of which should make anxious the friends of free
constitutional government.

"A new broom sweeps clean. A temporary National
Prohibition law as a war measure may be effective. It is
urged to stimulate war production in the emergency, and
to take temptation from our soldiers, though it is doubtful
whether the serious loss to the National Revenues, which
it will entail, may not outweigh the actual benefits. The
immediately useful operation of such a law, or of a new state
prohibition law, is not convincing evidence of its ultimate
tendency and result. The community must summer and
winter it for years. After the law-abiding members of the
business go out of the business, and a complete readjustment
follows, the pressure for violation and law execution in communities where the law is not popular will be constant and
increasing. The reaching out of the great central power to
brush the door-steps of local communities, far removed
geographically and politically from Washington, will be
irritating in such states and communities, and will be a
strain upon the bonds of the national union. It will produce
variation in the enforcement of the law. There will be loose
administration in spots all over the United States, and a
politically inclined National Administration will be strongly
tempted to acquiesce in such a condition. Elections will
continuously turn on the rigid or languid execution of the
liquor law, as they do now in prohibition states. The ever
present issue will confuse and prevent clear and clean cut
popular decisions on the most important national questions,

# Appendix

and the politics of the nation will be as demoralized as the politics of states have been through this cause. The issue will never be settled.

"The theory that the national government can enforce any law will yield to the stubborn circumstances, and a federal law will become as much a subject of contempt and ridicule in some parts of the nation as laws of this kind have been in some states. We are acting now under the heroic impulse of a war, which stirs our feelings and makes us think that we can have a millennium of virtue and self-sacrifice for the future. This is a fundamental error. I profoundly deprecate having our constitutional structure seriously amended by a feverish enthusiasm, which will abate to neglect and laxity in many states as the years go on. If, through the abnormal psychology of war, the 36 states are induced to approve a national prohibition amendment now, we can never change it, though a great majority of the people may come later to see its utter failure. Thirteen prohibition states can always be counted on to prevent a retracing of the foolish step. We shall thus hang a permanent millstone around our necks.

"Individual self-restraint, the influence of improved social standards and criticism, and the restrictions enforced by employers of labor for industrial reasons, have probably had more to do with moderating the evils of intoxication than statute law. I would not minimize, however, the advantage of the removal of the temptations of access to liquor by law, when the law is backed by local public opinion and can be enforced.

"Nor is my conviction affected by any sympathy with those who are engaged in the manufacture or sale of intoxicating liquors. It is now nearly half a century ago since the supreme court's interpretation of the federal constitution warned everyone engaged in the business that he invested a capital therein at the full risk of being declared unlawful and of the consequent loss that future legislation might entail. Moreover, the demoralizing political power which saloon keepers and liquor manufacturers sought and wielded to protect their business from proper regulation, and the defiance they bid to reasonable public opinion, roused the just indignation of the electorate. Many have voted, and now vote, for prohibition merely to destroy the power of the saloon in politics, without regard to any other consideration. The saloon keepers taught the anti-saloon league how to fight, and the latter has learned the lesson well and applied it, and often without any more scruples as to the method or means than its teachers. The liquor dealer thus is 'hoist with his own petard.'

"I have never concealed my views on this subject, and it is a matter in which one should speak out. An intensely active minority in favor of adopting an unwise policy, may win through the failure of the members of the majority, though opposed to the policy, publicly to declare themselves and to take the trouble to give effect to their opinions by their votes. A minority like this, conceiving that it is moved by a moral issue, loses its sense of proportion and sacrifices every other issue, no matter how vital to the nation. Such a minority visits with its condign punishment all public servants who oppose it on this issue, however useful to the state they may be. I would not impeach the high-minded motives of the great body of those who support national prohibition. It does awaken one's protest, however, to note the manner in which the ordinary type of politician becomes a prohibitionist because he fears the balance of power that an active political minority may wield against his political fortunes. In the past he may have been subservient to the liquor dealers. In the present his practices may completely refute the sincerity of the principles he advocates, but he, and men of his ilk, would recklessly and selfishly hurry us into an irretrievable national blunder.

"The regulation of the sale and use of intoxicating liquor should be retained by the states. They can experiment and

# Appendix

improve. They have full power, and the federal government has helped them by making it a federal offense to import liquor into their borders, if they forbid it. If the power of regulation is irrevocably committed to the general government, the next generation will live deeply to regret it.

"For these reasons, therefore, first, because a permanent national liquor law in many communities will prove unenforceable for lack of local public sympathy; second, because attempted enforcement will require an enormous force of federal policemen and detectives, giving undue power to a sinister and partisan subordinate of the national administration, and third, because it means an unwise structural change in the relations between the people of the states and the central government, and a strain to the integrity of the union, I am opposed to a national prohibition amendment.

Sincerely yours,<br>William H. Taft"

# INDEX

# Index

# Index

Spanish-American War, 31
Staples, Seth P., 29
Staples Law School, 29, 30
States' rights, 70, 75
Stokes, Anson Phelps, 2, 3, 5, 9, 15, 18, 34, 35, 39, 104, 110, 112, 137
Stokes Foundation, 77
Stone, Harlan Fiske, 76
Story, Joseph, 60
Superior Court judge, 10
Surbeck, Leighton H., 127
Swan, Thomas W., 61, 62, 64, 67, 123, 126–127

TAFT, Alphonso, 11, 142
Taft, Charles P., 2
Taft, Horace D., 2, 85, 110, 115, 120
Taft, William Howard: admitted to Ohio Bar, 10; attendance at Faculty meetings, 32, 63–64; automobile, 91, 111; books borrowed from Yale libraries, 81; chuckle, 109; church attendance, 99; citizen of New Haven, 91; College teacher, 38; Dean, Cincinnati University Law School, 11, 63–64, 67; death, 140; declined to preach sermons, 36; diet, 117; Fellow of Yale Corporation, 9, 124; fiftieth reunion of his college class, 137–139; final examinations, 53; health, 114–120, 139; height, 117; humor, 109–114; income, 1, 13; law books, 80; law teacher, 11, 46, 63–64, 67; method of teaching, 40, 42, 51; non-drinker, 116; non-smoker, 116; objectivity, 44; planted trees on Green, 94; portraits of, 27; Professor of Real Property, Cincinnati, 11; proposed as Yale Law School Dean, 63; public offices held, 10, 68; reasons for not practicing law, 1; Red Cross National Chairman, 97; relations with College Faculty, 32; relations with Law Faculty, 59–67; religion, 36–37, 138; residences in New Haven, 4, 88–90; salary, 3, 13, 49; size of Law School classes, 50; tardy at classes, 38; tolerance, 31; weight, 114, 118
Taft, Mrs. William Howard, 18, 19, 37, 95, 121, 137, 138
Taft Law Library Endowment Fund, 142, 143
*Taft Papers on League of Nations*, 87
Talbot, N. S., 20
Taxes, 91
Ten-minute papers, 41, 42, 51
Thacher, James, 118
Thayer, James Bradley, 47, 65
Thurston, Edward S., 62, 64
Tiggs, D., 17
Tilson, John Q., 97
Treaty ratification, 76, 86
Tuttle, Emerson, 40

ULLMAN, I. M., 5, 24, 92
Ullman, Mrs. I. M., 98
Undergraduate marriages, 32
Unitarians, 36, 37, 94, 138
*The United States and Peace*, 84
United States Circuit judge, 10
United States Constitution, 7, 26
United States *v.* Heinszen Co., 54, 55
United Workers Boys Club, 94
Universalists, 38
University of Chicago, 73
University of Minnesota, 39, 78
University of Rochester, 77
University of Toronto, 73
University of Virginia, 73

VERSAILLES Treaty, 13
Veto power, 75
Villard, Oswald Garrison, 115